Edward Everett Hale

Sermons of the winter

Edward Everett Hale

Sermons of the winter

ISBN/EAN: 9783337257873

Printed in Europe, USA, Canada, Australia, Japan

Cover: Foto ©Lupo / pixelio.de

More available books at **www.hansebooks.com**

SERMONS OF THE WINTER.

BY

EDWARD E. HALE, D.D.,

Minister of the South Congregational Church, Boston.

AUTHOR OF

"IN HIS NAME," "DAILY BREAD," "EVERY-DAY SERMONS."

———◆———

BOSTON:
J. STILMAN SMITH & CO.,
3 HAMILTON PLACE.
1893.

Copyright, 1893,
BY J. STILMAN SMITH & COMPANY.

SERMONS OF THE WINTER.

EVERY working minister knows the convenience of printing sermons. One has more parishioners far away from home than hear him in the church. And it sometimes happens that those who heard want to refresh their memories.

"Printed at the request of some that heard," is the familiar statement on the title-page of the sermons of a century ago, which seem as quaint to us as these will a century hence.

I have been, therefore, very glad to print these sermons, week by week almost, as they were delivered in the South Congregational Church, between Sunday, September 18, 1892, and Sunday, June 11, 1893. The quiet line of winter life in Boston was broken, once and again, by events which touched to the heart the whole community in which we live. But most of the sermons are not what people call "occasional," but refer to those needs of human life which never change.

EDWARD E. HALE.

SOUTH CONGREGATIONAL CHURCH,
    BOSTON, June 26, 1893.

CONTENTS.

	PAGE
THE CHURCH AND THE WORLD	3
THE FIRST CHURCH OF CHRIST	17
LIFE HID WITH GOD	29
THE PERFECT SUNDAY-SCHOOL	41
TO GLORIFY GOD	59
WHITTIER, CURTIS, LONGFELLOW	71
"'TIS FIFTY YEARS SINCE"	85
PERSONAL RELIGION	102
MODERN IDOLATRY	113
TO ENJOY HIM FOREVER	126
TRUTH	137
HOW TO USE THE BIBLE	148
LIGHT OF THE WORLD	161
PHILLIPS BROOKS	174
CREEDS AND LIFE	187
LAW OF LOVE	199
CHRISTIAN MYSTICS	210
FAILURE AND STRENGTH	223
PALM SUNDAY	235
EASTER	247
MANHOOD	258
THE WILL OF GOD	271
SUMMER SERVICE	282

THE CHURCH AND THE WORLD.

"Go ye, therefore, and make disciples of all the nations."
MATTHEW xxviii. 19.

FIVE weeks ago this morning I joined in the service of the Established Church of England on my last Sunday in England. It was in the Cathedral of Canterbury, so grand and beautiful. Canterbury claims to be the seat of the earliest Saxon Church in England, and from which the Archbishop, Primate of England, takes his title. The full cathedral service was conducted with dignity and with feeling — that sense, indeed, of what worship is, which one does not always observe in the cathedral service of England. To my great joy, Dr. Fremantle, one of the canons of Canterbury, ascended the pulpit when we came to the sermon. You have often heard me speak of him here as being, in my estimate, the first preacher in the Church of England now. I think few of her most intelligent clergymen would be surprised at that estimate. He gave out this text. He read it, as I do, from the Revised Version — a thing to be noticed, because although that version was made under the authority of the Church of England, it is not very often heard in her churches. He proceeded, without the least preface, to a discussion of the duty of the

Church in our day, broad and even radical; practical to the last degree, and sublimely indifferent to the conventional standards of any narrow theology. I am not going to repeat the sermon now, though I could do so, and it might profit all of us. His subject in the series of sermons, of which this is one, was the immediate duty of the Church of Christ in our time. He did not say that it was to save the souls of those who heard the gospel. He did not say that it was to present that gospel to the heathen. He did not say that it was to preserve, with honor, the memories of what passed in Palestine in the time of Tiberius. He did not say that it was to preserve and strengthen this or that organization with this or that set of officers and of routine, and he did not so much as allude to the fact that more than half the pulpits of Christendom would have stated the function of the Church in some such conventional phrase. No; he passed calmly and silently by all such conventionalities and commonplaces. "The business of the Church," he said, "is to make more spiritual the daily life of the time."

The statement is admirable for its simplicity. It is broad enough to be a good working statement. You may say it is more needed in England than it is here; and possibly it is more needed among that half of the people of England who would say that they belonged to the Church of England, than to that other half who are called

Non-conformists. Of such detail he said nothing. He merely applied his broad principle to the special matter he had in hand, in that particular sermon of a series.

Now, there is no one here to whom this statement seems in the least radical or unfamiliar. The Church of Christ exists to spiritualize the every-day life of the time. Any of us here would have said something of this sort had he been asked yesterday to say why churches exist, or why the church should be maintained. I quote Dr. Fremantle's statement, not as if it were new, but because we may take it — shall I say, as self-evident — as a statement that does not need proof, — a statement which will be widely agreed to. Such a proposition, coming from such a man, in such a place, makes a convenient "departure," as seamen say, for our winter voyage, on which we enter with this morning's service. It is not what Dr. Hale says, it is not what the Unitarians say, from which we will start. It is not the gospel of our left wing, or of the light skirmishers, who make the advance of the army of God. It is the statement which slow and conservative England makes. The pulpit in the choir of the Primate's Cathedral of Canterbury makes it, that the Church of God exists to give more spirit in every day to the every-day life of the time.

This is, beyond doubt, what the Saviour of mankind meant and asked for when he sent those eleven men off on the great affair. This is what he means when he tells them to make disciples of all the nations.

———

On this side of the ocean we have an advantage for the discussion of these duties which they have not in Canterbury. Our practical definition of the word "Church" is larger than theirs. This country was made by Englishmen, who crossed the ocean because they believed that the power of the Church belonged to all her people ; while the government of England held that it belonged to the clergy. We have fought that matter through, and everybody here lives on that principle except the Roman Catholic Church and a few of its imitators. We have not any such words to define, or other such foundation to lay.

But all the more have we to study the duty which every man, woman, and child has in this business of lifting up the spiritual life of the community. To-day — as we meet here again — I have much more to ask, than how in this house we can conduct this service this winter, or what I and my assistants can do about our charities or hospitalities. Our business to-day is to find out how each of us separately, and all of us together, can carry forward this business of the Church. We are born into it, and we cannot get out of it. We can see in every hour that there is a great deal to be done. Prize-fights, cholera, everything that passes in the community, show the need of lifting the community to a higher spiritual life. Who is to lift it? The Church. Who is the Church? You and I. Then our inquiry is a very definite inquiry as to what, to you and me, is a very practical affair.

And the answer is not far away. It is not in the heavens that we should fly for it, nor in the depths that we should dive for it. It is hidden in the question.

FIRST of all, the idea of Duty: that I must do this duty or that, as it comes next my hand — this is the Prophet Word. The detail of Duty may settle itself, but the word *ought*, or the reality *ought* — beaten into the public mind by blows, flashed in as by electricity, sung in by poets, agreed in by men of talk, best of all shown in daily life by men and women who do what they ought to do — this sense of Right changes the town or the land from being a hell to being a heaven.

So is it that you and I, if we would uplift this people, are to live not by what amuses us, or by what pleases us, — not for sugar-candy, or sunny prospects, or elegant art, or seeking a shilling's pay for sixpence's work. No; we are to do the duty that comes next our hand. As we do that, so that men know what duty is, we lift up the community from a place among the slums of the universe to its own place in the kingdom of heaven — we spiritualize the world in which we live.

We bring an Indian from his tepee on the plains and show him our marvels. Perhaps a wizard in Salamanca's cave rings a bell in Notre Dame, — and we ask the savage to express his surprise. But such things are not the great marvel. The great marvel of high civilization, and that which works the little marvels, is the loyal obedience which those who lead the life give, and will give, to law. For instance, at seven in the morning a clock strikes; at once a hundred whistles blow, to show that the world has turned seven twenty-fourths of her way since midnight, since Boston was just opposite the sun. And at that instant so many trains start obedient from so many stations; so many thousand men and women go to so many places where they are needed; so many keys are placed in so many locks; so many doors are opened, and the duties of a hundred thousand lives begin. Put that in contrast with the easy indifference of my savage's life, in which he does what he likes to do at the moment he happens to think of it, or leaves it all alone if he do not happen to fancy it. Of a voyage across the ocean, in what is a little world, a ship snapped off from the shore, as they say the moon was flung from the earth when all was yielding and plastic; in that ship the miracle is the consent in duty of the hundred and fifty men who all together drive her to her port.

The stoker, half-naked, wheels his coal for four hours from the bunker to the furnace. At the moment when his four hours are over, he knows that another stoker will appear, ready to take the barrow for four hours more. Perhaps those men do not know each other's names; they hardly nod to each other as they change hands at the barrow. But each man knows that the other is in his duty, and that that duty will be fulfilled. From those laborers, who carry the coal in which God has packed away the fire of the sun, as it blazed a hundred thousand years ago upon some old fern-field, — from those men up to the thoughtful, prayerful, skilful captain, who is awake at midnight, while I am sleeping in my berth, that he may be sure on just what square mile of God's world that ship is voyaging, — the sense of duty is at the bottom of the hearts of those hundred and fifty men. What is more, that duty is fulfilled. This motive, that motive, another motive, are mixed in together; but law, and the obedience to law; duty, and the determination to perform duty; "ought," and all that "ought" stands for, are holding those men each in his place, and each place fits in with each other place, each pinion with each rack. Of which the issue is that the ship is driven forward, and at the preordained moment of the preordained day arrives in her port, because this duty has been done. Now, that is the moral lesson of the value of duty well done; obedience to the stern voice of the " daughter of Jove." That moral lesson is the same when the stoker does his duty, when the quartermaster does his duty, when the captain does his. And you and I, as we address ourselves this winter to Christ's work, in giving spiritual life to this community, are to remember that our first business in that affair is in the regular, cheerful, cordial, discharge of our special daily duty. To be in our places precisely in time, to do the work that is given us in good temper and not in bad, to speak the words we have to say kindly and not harshly, to show to all men and women, and angels and devils, that our duty is the first thing, is the central thing, is the great reality. This is our first affair in this gospel which is given to our charge.

2. And the second is like unto it. We are to do this duty, whatever it is, in the nursery, in the school-room, at the furnace like the stoker, or in the chart-room with the captain, — we are to do it in love for all the rest. Simply, it is not a mechanical affair, as when the wheel of my clock is forced into its place by the swing of a pendulum. No; it is the voluntary determination of my own independent thought, that I will live, not for myself, but for those whom God has given me. Simply, that is, I act as a god acts, and not as a thing. And whosoever is downcast or dismayed

because his place in this great hierarchy is so humble, or, worse than that, because he has not found what his place is, has to remember that, be it in this place or in that place, if he will speak or act, or go or sit still, in love for those who are around him, he performs the full apostle's duty. He works the full apostolic miracle. In that love of the brethren he opens the eyes of the blind and the ears of the deaf; he wakes the dead from death, and makes them walk as the children of the living God. That poor emigrant mother whom I see in the steerage, crouching down to protect her baby against the sweep of the north-east wind, stealing the shawl from her own head that she may wind it around her child, may or may not put her child to sleep, may or may not make the child's life happier or more comfortable; but in her own self-sacrifice, in her own indifference to ease or personal desire, she is doing her part. Her light is upon the candlestick, and all men and women who see it may well wish that their light shone before men as well. Which is to say that, in the spirit of love, though one only try to help those who are close at hand, and cannot see where he succeeds in trying, in the spirit of love itself, he is lifting up the whole world, and making it, as I said, a part of the kingdom of heaven.

So that this is our second lesson for our apostleship. We are not to be satisfied with the hard performance of the thing which is to be done, as if we had brought in the kingdom when we have piled up a hundred cents to make a dollar, or sixteen ounces to make a pound. This kingdom of heaven to which we are to lift the Boston in which we live, is not merely a well-adjusted machine; it is not an affair of axles and cranks and cogs and measurements. It is a kingdom alive with the very life of God; it is strong with God's strength, because it lives with his life. And when one has said this, one has said that it comes where there is love, and does not come without it. For it is true of this little section of the kingdom as it is true of the universe, that "love is heaven, and heaven is love."

You and I, if we mean to be apostles to all the world of absolute religion, are to do every day the duty that comes next our hand — yes, with the precision with which the moving stars do theirs. And we are not to do it simply as the moving stars, dead and unconscious, do. No; we are to do it as those who love each other, and who live and move and have their being under the infinite empire of such perfect love.

3. All this is necessary to say, I am afraid, because even literature in its common voices, because, alas! the pulpit in its more frequent appeals, second a certain cross-purpose of the human intellect, in which people talk of "high and low," in which people talk of "strong and weak." The heresy comes in, which discourages

Dorcas, who is at work with her needle, because it praises some Aaron Burr who has a sharp and cunning intellect. The heresy comes in, which makes me repine because I can do nothing but bring a load of wood to market, when I read of the sway and power of a man like Whittier, who has written songs for a nation. Now, I must not let myself be swept away by this heresy. It is merely the voice of the flesh and of the devil. The infinite truth is, as the Lord Jesus showed, and every apostle of his has shown, that each of us who chooses to enter into the divine life, can work the divine and infinite miracles with the full power of the living God. In that miracle there is no great and no little; there is no long and no short; there is no high and no low. We work it because we are God's children; it is because we, too, are creative forces. "My Father worketh hitherto and I work." That is its text and axiom. The present God sends me to this or that work of love. Who am I that I should call it common or unclean? The present God has given me power for to-day's endeavor. Who am I, to whine at night because I do not know what stone that endeavor has lifted, or how it has set forward His infinite work for His children? He is with me, and I am with Him. It is the service which is perfect freedom. He and I went about this affair together to-day, and because we went about it together, we know it will succeed.

Practically speaking, the mission to which we are sent, which the text happens to express in words which were critical when they were spoken, is so absolutely infinite that it gives grandeur to all duty, it enlarges all life to the very utmost. Because I am an apostle of God, I am lifted above meanness and anxiety, I am even lifted above the fear of failure. I may throw aside — on the right hand and on the left hand — all this contempt for my particular position, so only I glorify that work with the glories of love for my neighbor, and do that work in the spirit of absolute loyalty to the present law. In such endeavor as that, and in such enterprise, there is no fear that I shall be satisfied with vulgar tastes or beastly appetites. Thus, if I go about that infinite work, in that spirit of perfect love, I cannot poison this body with one or another stimulant or narcotic; I cannot debase this hand to one or another fraud or forgery; I cannot coop up this body in one or another prison. Once let me take the sense of apostleship, once see that I am sent about the same business that Jesus Christ was sent about, that he and his Father have sent me into the world as his Father sent him into the world, and I shall insist from day to day on living life higher than the life of the flesh, and on looking farther than a man can look who only opens the window yonder and is satisfied with the view of the street. I shall insist on looking beyond this earth upon infinite horizons. I shall insist in my workshop on tracing out what I do into its infinite results, and finding the infinite purpose with which God has set me to that effort. I shall not read or study without forecasting, though it be dimly, what is the future which is to come from such words as are written upon this page. I shall not, indeed, go or come in my daily duty without asking, at least, how that duty is to be done in the twentieth century, and in the centuries after that, — how it is that men are to rise on wings like eagles, to run without being weary, and to walk without being faint. And I shall be a true apostle of this gospel, though I be a shoemaker at the bench, or a coal-heaver on the wharf, if, when Tuesday follows Monday, I am doing that present work with a larger sense of its dignity and its result. Simply, my life of every day is to be a larger life in its purpose than the life of the day before, if I am loyally to accept the injunction of the great apostleship.

4. That is a critical and dramatic scene when, on a mountain in Galilee, Jesus sends off these eleven disciples, wondering and dazed, on the errand which encompasses the world. Was it the mountain of the beatitudes? Was it the mountain of the transfiguration? No wonder that the painters reproduce it. No wonder that in legend and in history we try to show how the eleven obeyed, — Thomas in far-off India; Andrew in frozen Scythia; Peter crucified in Rome.

But the scene to-morrow morning is as critical, and to an angel's eye might be as dramatic, as you and I shall go out on the same affair. Of these apostles here, — these men and women, — how many believe they have this mission, and how many are thinking of fame or of merchandise only; of the dinner with which the day shall close, or the profit of the day's delving and forging? These last must be crossed off our list — they are not apostles. But there are — more than eleven here — yes, many more — who know that they are sent. They are "those sent;" that is, they are "apostles." And this Boston, because they are sent, shall be a part of the kingdom of heaven. Because they are sent, these people in Boston shall be made disciples of the gospel of glad tidings. Some there are who can sing its strains, some there are who can tell its history, some there are who can repeat its words — its preface. But, if there were none such, there is not one of us here but can do the duty next his hand, as a son of God may do it. He **can** do it in gentle, perfect love, as Mary Mother did hers to the baby on her knees. He can so do this loving duty as one who lives in the kingdom of heaven now.

He who thus enters on to-morrow's work, engaging thus in his Father's business, is in that moment an apostle.

THE FIRST CHURCH OF CHRIST.

"For the Jews have no dealings with the Samaritans."
JOHN iv. 9.

I TRIED, not long ago, to illustrate the contrast between Jerusalem and this Sychar, — between Jewish and Samaritan formalism; and at the same time to condense, from two thousand years of history, something of the bitterness which tinges the words, "For the Jews have no dealings with the Samaritans."

We have idolized the books themselves so much, that, even in pulpit reading, these contrasts hardly appear. I cannot often enough express my horror at our thinking all Bible words good, and all Bible people sacred, in a uniform fashion. Really, in the average thought, Barabbas and Caiaphas are elevated to much the same plane, in this stupid idolatry, as that on which we place Paul or John. But, in face of this habit, I shall try this morning to carry farther the contrast between Jerusalem and Sychar.

If we were reading of the life of President Lincoln, and in one chapter of the book read that he met Governor Dix, of New York, at the capitol in Albany, and in the next chapter that he met a black woman at Harper's Ferry, we should at once expect the methods of handling the subject to differ, — we should look for, and we should find, the difference. But the average reader of the New Testament neither looks for nor finds any such difference here, when Jesus parts from a senator in Jerusalem and meets an outcast of Samaria. "Why should there be any difference? It is all one whether this woman has any name or does not have any name. Why should she have a name? Why should her name be written down? It is all one whether Nicodemus is a senator or a fish-woman. Truth is truth, and if the Saviour had anything to say, he would say it to one, as he would say it to the other. Such is the average stupid habit of plunging on, in Bible reading.

The distinction really is, between the capital of Israel and a valley of Gentiledom. It is the difference between organized religion and unorganized come-outerism. It is the difference between talk with a nobleman and talk with a peasant.

Once more: this conversation at Sychar is one connected whole, reported long years after, very likely, but standing wholly by itself. You can publish it alone, and it explains itself. Some of the critics have guessed that each of the seven portions of the fourth Gospel was written by itself, and published, as we say, by itself. It is certain that that might have been. It is as if both parties knew that they should not meet again, — the Samaritans and the Saviour. There is hardly another chapter in the four Gospels which you could so dissect and make it explain itself. It was for this quality that I once called it here " the title-page of the gospel."

It teaches to the nameless woman and her nameless friends four central lessons, — an abridgment in four texts, I might say, of the gospel doctrine.

1. In the very fact that he speaks to them, the whole notion of a peculiar people of God — and of all special revelations — gives way. They are not Jews — they are people of Samaria. They do not claim what Nicodemus claimed in Jerusalem for himself and a circle of noblemen. They care nothing for the son of David. So far as they hang by the race of Abraham, theirs is the line of Ephraim. All Jewish partisanship, all Pharisaic pride, all notion that God loves one people more than another, is to be set aside in the work of a Saviour who first announces himself to a woman of Samaria. Whatever else this new religion is, it is not the religion of one race of men. It is, indeed, to prove itself the religion of mankind.

2. The woman begins talking about ritual, as most people do to-day when they find themselves in presence of a religious teacher. And this teacher sweeps all that away. " God is a spirit, and they that worship Him must worship Him in spirit and in truth." Here is an end of all forms of God or images of God, — of all visible representations of God. No more Phidian Jove.

No more Jehovah walking in the garden in the cool of the day. It is the fashion of people now to say that they doubt the personality of God. By which they seem to mean that they have given up the ideas of His stretching out His hand, or shadowing with His wings. All which Jesus Christ tried to make them give up in this title-page of positive religion. God is a Spirit. The Holy Spirit, which creates and informs, it is God. They who choose to worship Him, or wish to worship Him, are not to worship Him by tithes or sacrifices. It is not by killing doves or oxen. It is not by processions or by the sound of trumpets. Unless they worship in spirit and in truth, there is no worship. *If* they worship in spirit and in truth, one form will speak their purpose as well as another.

3. This Infinite Spirit — which directs the motion of planets and compels the sun to shine, which is in all space — is here. It is here now. Wherever spirit is, this spirit of God is. We men, who are spirits clad in veils, belong to it, and are of the same nature. There is an "Identity of essence in all Spiritual Being, and all Spiritual Life."[1] So that man is not to count himself apart from God, or God apart from him. No; he lives in God, moves in God, and in God has his being. He partakes his Father's nature. Jesus said this to the Samaritan woman and her

---

[1] A phrase of Dr. James Walker.

companions when he said so distinctly that God the Spirit sends him and anoints him. "I who speak unto thee am he."

4. She has the half-heathen idea of her Messiah as of a messenger sent from a far-off king on a distant throne. He is to come with heralds and body-guards; he is to prostrate Rome, and he is to tell us all things. "He is coming, and he will tell us all things, — he, the anointed."

"Woman, he has come. I who am talking to you am he. Dusty and tired with my journey, with no herald before me and no train behind me, glad to drink from your pitcher because I am faint, — all the same, I am the child of God, and His present messenger to you. I who speak unto you am he."

I do not wonder that the painters are so fond of the subject. But one wishes that they did not care so much for the mountains and the well, and cared more for him and for her. That he should have swept away all her prejudices — prejudices born from twenty centuries; that he, a dusty, tired, lonely wayfarer, should in five minutes make her know that he is God's son, and is speaking God's word to her, — this shows what manner of man he was, and what it is in him which makes him Saviour of the world.

And she, on her side? That in those five minutes every cloud should have rolled away from her heaven; that all dust of man's travel, and all smoke from the sacrifices of priests, should have been cleared away, so that she can see that her God visits her and helps her, and that she is a child of God! Let the artist express that emancipation, and we shall know what is meant when they say, "All things are become new." This is what the words "New Testament" mean.

In a word, she saw what Nicodemus could not see. When this same word had come to him to say, "You must be born again;" "I don't think we can," was his reply. But she went up into the village and told her people that this man had told her everything.

His other disciples join him and the Samaritans from the village. He stays two days in this Sychar,—the typical city of the Gentile, to the eye of a bigoted Jew. And here he establishes the first church in the world. Many of the Samaritans believe on him, because they have seen him and heard him. "We have heard him ourselves, and know that this is indeed the Saviour of the world." What they heard in those two days we cannot tell; but the central thing in it—to be remembered when all this was written down at the end of threescore years or more—was this: "My meat is to do the will of Him that sent me, and to finish His work." "The fields are white to the harvest, though it is early springtime." The doctrine of this gospel to the Samaritans is that man is of God's nature, and that he is a fellow-worker together with God.

In one and another mood of meditation — looking backward and looking forward — we ask ourselves what Jesus Christ would do for us to-day. What is his mission to this time? Or what would he say to me if my ears heard the plashing of Galilee's wave? So far does this meditative mood affect men, that there are large groups of Christians who dream of a Second Advent near, and are looking for a speedy arrival of the Saviour in this time. A clergyman of the English church told me that a thousand of his fellow-ministers hoped for this. And I knew men, thirty years ago, who were so sure that Christ in bodily presence would settle our Civil War for us, that they did not think they need themselves volunteer. Suppose he came, — what has he to say?

I dare say this no-named woman of Sychar had asked herself the same question that morning.

This is sure, that our answer would come as hers did. Perhaps our surprise would be as great as hers. Let us hope our eyes would open as quickly as hers. It is not in a chariot of fire descending from the clouds that her Saviour comes. It is not with legions of white-winged angels, or the clarion tones of cherubim before him and behind him, that he comes. It is a lonely, tired man — dusty with travel, and sitting on the wellside, — whom she finds, and who is to tell her all things. So you and I will hear our gospel, not in any voice from the sky, and not in any legend written among the stars, but in the midst of the dust, and sweat, and travail of to-day.

And this is the first lesson that he has for to-day, as it was then: that there is no peculiar people and no separate religion. Pure religion and undefiled is for everybody, — black, white, gray, red, and brown. Nobody is predestinated to it, except that all are born to it. His religion is universal religion. It is absolute religion. In the midst of the modern theologies, which talk of this man as elected to salvation, and that man as elected to damnation, this Son of God walks in, chooses some reprobate of the by-ways for his confidant, and announces a universal religion.

Now, as then, whoever he met would, most likely, put the old question: "Please, where should you like to have me go to church? Shall I go to the Cathedral yonder? Or would you prefer that I should go to Clarendon street, or to the Tremont-street Methodist, or to the Tremont-street Congregational, or to Trinity? Or, I believe your people say that on Arlington street or Berkeley street is the place where men ought to worship?"

After eighteen or nineteen centuries the reply is just what it was. Woman, it is not here, it is not there. It is not the place of worship: it is the quality of worship. "God is a spirit, and they that worship Him must worship Him in spirit and in truth."

And how shall he worship? With this prayer

or that hymn? With these articles or that creed? Answers now as then: Look on the fields! They are white to harvest, — January, March, July, or November, it is all one, they are always white to harvest. God did not finish His world. He is here now. He is in and with His children now — that with Him His children may go harvesting now. Those join in worship of Him rightly, who rightly and bravely go to work with Him. They show they are truly His, if they go about their Father's business. And this is the sum and substance of pure religion.

Renan says in his brilliant way that if the Christian world ever wishes to replace by authentic monuments those apocryphal sanctuaries which the piety of the Dark Ages has left to it, it will build its temple on the heights of Nazareth. "Christendom," he says, "should build the grand temple where all Christians can unite in prayer, at that point, whence the movement which made Christendom rayed forth at its beginning."

But if the world seeks a monument of the place where was first proclaimed the truth which has made the world of to-day, that monument exists already in the old well at Sychar. This same writer, sometimes so impertinent in his patronage, is humbled before the central words here spoken. "Jesus spoke here, for the first time, the word on which will stand the building of the eternal religion. Here and then he founded the pure worship, without date and without country, which will be the religion of all noble souls to the end of time. The religion of that word and that day is not only the religion good for humanity, it is absolute religion. And if other planets have inhabitants endowed with reason and the sense of right, their religion cannot differ from this of Jacob's well. Grant that men fall back from it; that they only cling to the ideal for an instant. It was a flash — this word of his — in the thick darkness; and in eighteen hundred years the eyes of mankind (alas! of an infinitely small fraction of mankind) are used to it. All the same, full light will come; and after the full circle of wandering, man will come back to this word as to the immortal expression of its faith and its hope."

I said here once, that the four mottoes for the new frieze of a new church of the Good Samaritan might well be these four texts:

"*Not in this mountain, nor at Jerusalem*," because ours is a universal religion.

"*God is a spirit.*" This for its statement of God.

"*I who speak to you am he.*" This for its statement of Christ, — that he is a weary wayfarer, sitting thirsty in the midst of his day's work.

"*My meat is to finish God's work, and I send you to the harvest.*" This for man's place and duty, because man is a child of God.

But you and I can do better things than to build the temple of Nazareth or design mottoes for the walls of a church at home. Paul's word is as true as it ever was, "Know ye not that the temple of God is holy, which temple ye are?" These texts are not for one place or another place. They are truths for you and me to carry wherever we go. This title-page to the gospel is not illustrated when we go on a pilgrimage to the vale of Sychar, when we sit in the shade of the well, and, in some broken tongue, talk to the Samaritans who are there to-day. No! It is when we lift up our eyes and look upon these fields that we illustrate it. It is when we go to work to accomplish our Father's work. It is when we thus bring to the Life of Lives, to the God who is the spirit of all life, the only worship, which is the worship of spirit and of truth. Then and only, we know what these words mean, "I that speak unto thee am he." They will speak in the midst of daily duty. He who speaks will be dusty and travel-worn; but when we have heard him for ourselves, we too shall know that this, indeed, is the Saviour of the world.

"Lift up your eyes and look upon the fields, for they are white already to harvest." If he said it there, in that narrow valley between Ebal and Gerizim, what would he have said here, as from our outlook he saw the Massachusetts of to-day? He need not bid you and me go out to all the world to proclaim his glad tidings: all the world comes to us. I do not know but I am speaking to some nobleman from Japan. I do not know but some Chinese boy has conquered this puzzling language so far that he can follow what I say. I do know that I have only to walk the streets to-morrow to meet men of all the great races of the world. If I could talk in Hebrew I might speak to the Jew who landed last week — not the worst of emigrants, let me say in passing, at a moment when it is the fashion to abuse him. I am to be asked, it seems, before the month is over, to welcome Eskimos from Labrador on their way to Chicago. And this is only a type, or specimen, illustrating that matchless hospitality by which a pure democracy like Massachusetts gives to all their due, Jew or Gentile, bond or free, and attracts within her charmed limits all sorts and conditions of men. When she built a church like this, she set a candle in a candlestick — set a city upon a hill, that all men might see her light; might see it and might come to it. And you and I are the wardens who tend that watch-fire. You and I are crews in the life-boat ready to put off into the breakers and rescue the shipwrecked pilgrim from other lands. You and I have received from holy fathers, and from mothers who prayed God that we might be true, the torch which is lighted for the blessing of the world. Who are we, that we should be false to such a trust, should fail to trim that torch and compel it to burn brighter? From hand to hand we give it gladly and sure to this waiting hereafter!

LIFE HID WITH GOD.

"Your life is hid with Christ in God." — COLOSSIANS iii. 3.

It is not the show or the outside which is really of the first import. Life, the motive power, is hidden.

Jesus himself feels this so intensely that you can see how much he is pained when people do not apprehend it. "Show us a sign from heaven," they say to him, exactly as outside people do now. It is just as sensational reporters, and other outside people, of all sorts, ask to see this or that, — which is hidden. And he says, so sadly, "Oh! it is an evil generation which seeks after a sign." And all the matters of Life, in just his spirit, tell you that Life is a secret. It is a secret, if you please, which you judge by the fruit. But power is hidden. And Paul means, with a certain reverence, to state this secrecy, when he says that with Christ our lives are hid in God. There is the secret force of Life. No eye can see it. No parable is sufficient for it. No words can fully express it. For it is in God. And no eye can see God; no parable is sufficient for Him, and no words can adequately describe Him. I can take a grain of mustard-seed, and under the microscope it is no longer small. But I cannot magnify it so far that I can see its life. I can dissect off the outer hull of the seed, I can split off the sides of the cell, I can point to the germ, and I can say to you, "That germ is alive." But the life is hidden, and I cannot show that to you. Or I can plant the seed, and fifty years after I can take you out into a thicket, and I can say, "Do you remember the mustard-seed we planted when we were boys?" That seed produced a large plant, and I came by here, and carefully shook out all the pods and dried them carefully, and planted them again. The next year, I hired a man to attend to it, and he had several pecks of mustard-seed. He formed a partnership with some other men, and they went into that business. And now, after fifty years, this whole region is devoted to raising mustard for the market. It all came from that one seed. I can show you all these results of the life of the mustard-seed, but I cannot show you its life. Its life is hid with God.

Whenever, therefore, a courageous girl writes to a friend a letter, in which she says, "I tried in vain to tell you yesterday where my pain came from, and what it was, and I failed. I have tried to write to-day, and I am not succeeding any better," she says to her correspondent just what Paul says, when he says our life is hid in God. The machinery is one thing, but the life is different. As different as spirit is from thing, is the life from the machinery. And the ordinary figures fail, because life-power is deeper down than are most of the forms of power which we see. I want to find the power which drives my steam-engine, and I go down into the cellar, to the boiler. There the heated steam rushes out and passes into the cylinder above. The engineer says, perhaps, "Here is our power." But he knows, and I know, that there is a secret which we do not see. If the steam escape, we can see it as it condenses. We can even measure its expansive force on our register. But what is the power of the steam? Why does it expand as the fire heats the water? Why? Ah! that we do not know. We do not see the why, when, or see the where. Some learned friend tells us that it is in the "correlation of forces." He says that heat always expands, and that this measure of heat has been packed away in this coal, and is liberated in the burning. So then we go to the coal-mine, and we ask Mr. Lesley where the coal got the heat; and he says, "Oh! it was packed away there a hundred thousand years ago, when this was a fever-bog. And the sun shone hotly here, and that fire of that ancient sun burns now under your boiler." And we thank him, and we go back a hundred thousand years, — for man is infinite, and he can go back and go forward, — and we say, "Please, Sun, where did you get this power which makes the water expand?" And the Sun is good-humored that morning, but he says, "You ought to know more than I do. I am the creature of God, you are the child of God. All I know is what I do. My power comes to me because it is His will." His life is hid in God.

It is because the central power of life is thus secret that we speak of our inner Life as we do. It is for this that we pray, as the Saviour prayed for us, in our best prayer, when we ask for Life more abundantly. It is not simply for a wide field of living. It is that the roots of life may succeed in striking deeper, and may draw in more and more of the infinite life of the universe for me, and my daily duties and daily pleasures. It is true that Youth starts, in its imitation of Omnipotence, with the feeling that it has quite life enough, — more than it knows what to do with. But just so soon as the larger purposes come in, — those ambitions which include infinite aims, — youth or maiden begins feeling for more than the first fountain supplies. We must have infinite resource. It is, in truth, the Life of God which comes to the rescue — what the Bible calls, the Holy Spirit. Sometimes people know what it is, and sometimes they do not. But always they know that it is. It is the inner Life, not the outer life. It is not the life of running or walking, of eating or drinking; nay, it is not the life of thinking, of remembering, or of talking. It is deeper down. It gives more power to thought, to talk, to walking, or to running. So I say, as one grows in experience, he does not train himself simply on the outside, that he may write a better hand, or speak better French, or that his memory may be more accurate, or his style more correct. He seeks the inner Life. And he succeeds when he obtains it, when his own life is hid with God.

So is it that the books which have most completely taken hold of the world, hold it now, and will hold it, are books of the inner Life. First of all, the Bible is especially such. People discuss it as if it were a book of history, or a book of detailed instruction in ethics, — and it is. But it did not get its hold on the world either as a book of history or a code of ethics. Nor is it so that it keeps that hold. That came because it is men's guide to come nearer God. "Nearer to thee, my God." You can hardly open it anywhere, that you do not find something which brings God right into your consciousness, — the present God, — the God who is the Life of man. As you read, your life begins to be hid in God. Thomas à Kempis' book, called "The Imitation of Christ," takes its name from being the same thing. As Jesus Christ lived in God, moved in God, referred to God as the fountain of all his Life, so this book would have you and me do, while we read it. In the midst of the ebb and flow of what we call literature, of this picture of our times, and that study of history, and that prophecy of the future, such a book as "The Imitation of Christ" refers to something wholly beneath their brilliancy or their striving. It stands for real power, real Life, the abundance of Life of those who live with God. This man who wrote it had drunk at the fountain.

Our religious habits are formed largely of Jewish models. I mean that our religious language is taken largely from Jewish books. The parables or metaphors which we use for help are largely taken from Jewish literature. Against the dangers of such figures of speech we must guard ourselves. Because Christ speaks, as Jacob spoke, of a ladder on which angels ascended and descended, we must not forget that God is a Spirit, and they that worship Him, worship in spirit. Because the Hebrews had a Holy of Holies, we must not think we have to go here or to go there. Dr. Johnson's translation of an old hymn says

"O Thou whose power o'er moving worlds presides,
On darkling man in pure effulgence shine."

It implies — and this is what we borrow from the Jews — that we are not any more sure that God presides on these moving worlds, than we are that He shines on darkling man. Now, the truth is, that we are sure that God speaks in our hearts. This native voice of Right is God: its real name is the Word of God. I could wish, therefore, sometimes, that on some happy island we might find a race of men where religious language began at that end. If their language framed itself in the happy experience of the answer to prayer, on the experience of God's reward when one has done well, on the certainty that when I sought God I found Him because I sought for Him with all my heart,—if we had religious language absolutely based on such certainties, I think we should be saved some of our present difficulties. This is sure, that they are all difficulties of language. We choose to speak of God as foreseeing, though we know He is " I AM," and lives without time. Then we say we cannot reconcile His foresight and our freedom,—which means that the poor language with which we spoke of Him has broken down.

But, however weak language may be, this is certain, that the man who has felt God's help in crisis knows it, and asks no further demonstration.

It is, indeed, pathetic to see how this simplest language of the gospel writers refers to the Saviour's daily and nightly habit. The men seem to have been awe-struck as they saw it. He went into the mountain to pray. He was away all night in prayer. There is that most childlike — one almost says clumsy — wish that they were like him. " Master, teach us to pray." So clear is it to them that his power is God's power, and that he has means of getting it which they do not understand. People are puzzled in just that way now. And the failure of all language — language being purely material, and of the outside — accounts for the puzzle. But now, when you see or hear the confidence in the hidden Life, you respect it, and you believe. An officer will say to you, "No, I do not want to argue about it, I do not talk about it much. But I tell you that when the signal gun fired I backed my horse round to our place at the head of the division, I ordered a charge, and the division charged. God Almighty was my help and strength in that moment. I know it was so." Such is the kind of testimony quiet men give you. The man's life was hid in God's. "I was abject in grief. I did not care to live another minute. Of a sudden God spoke to me. He said this was His affair — that He had His purpose. I believed Him — I believe Him." When a man looks you in the eye and says that to you, there is no need of other argument or an examination of testimony. It is to him an ultimate fact. He will not go behind it. He does not know where his purpose began or ended. He does not ask where God's purpose began or ended. His life was hid in God.

I know very well how it is that at this point one and another person will say to me that they do not in the least know what I am talking about. I have heard people say so a hundred times. They say this is all mystery. They say it cannot be explained. As to its being all mystery, I have no doubt of that. All the connections between spirit and body are mysterious. Of course the relations between spirit and spirit are. I do not say, and I wish nobody had ever said, that there is any cunningly framed multiplication-table in which God's action should be shown in one of the columns and men's action in one of the cross-rows, so that at the point where they met you could see the product of the communion or common action of the two.

On the other hand, precisely what I say is, that the communion of man with God is not to be explained in any of the arbitrary or mechanical forms. But what, then? That is not strange. You cannot explain to the man who cannot swim, what is the method of swimming, what is the buoyancy of the water, what it is to be borne up and swept along by it in its flow. While he stands there on the gravel of the shore, he cannot know anything about this. He must trust himself to the water, implicitly, absolutely, and without reserve, or he cannot believe in it, and cannot understand its power. No man can understand. No man can even imagine what his sensations will be in his flight with a balloon, so long as he stands upon the earth without trusting himself to the air; what it is to see the earth recede, to see it form itself in a cup beneath one, as one floats, all unconscious of motion, and looks down. We can talk about this, but till one fairly trusts himself to the air, he does not feel it, conceive it, or know it. And so in the communions of human life, to a man who has lived along through youth and early manhood, without finding the other half of his life; without knowing what it is to have his heart-life rounded out and completed by a union with that other half, which is somewhere, and which belongs to him, — it is idle to talk of that communion or completeness.

Now to him who lingers on the beach, knowing nothing of swimming, you say that he must trust himself to the wave, he must try the great experiment, and see what it is to be buoyed up by it and swept along. And that is what, not you or I, but the Lord Jesus himself, and every voice of God Himself, say to those who have not tried the great experiment of losing their will in God's will, of hiding their life in His life. The birth of Christ, the life of Christ, and his death, were all for this end, — that you and I, and all men, might be willing to trust ourselves to the present love of God. Every martyr who has bled, every prophet who has spoken, every miracle of God's love, every victory of His power, the whole course of Christian history, the whole unfolding of His will, as it has appeared in the affairs of men, — all of these together are harmonious voices in His great appeal to us: that we, too, try the great experiment. He would have us give up our little separate purposes enough to work by His great purpose when He calls upon us. He would have our outside, selfish lives die out so that in our real Lives, our eternal Lives, we may be hid in God.

The language of the whole Epistle to the Colossians is as gorgeous and fanciful as is the "Arabian Nights." They had their own superstitions of genii, and afrites, and princes, and powers of the air; and Paul, who knew them through and through, was born, indeed, among their neighbors, takes them on their own terms and talks to them in their own way. This is hardly a violent figure — speaking in such enthusiasm to such men and women — by which he compares the change which Christianity made in their condition to the change wrought by death itself. He says, "They have changed from the life of beasts to that of God's children." Their old lusts, those bodily passions and desires, are done with. You have flung them off as a caterpillar flings off his chrysalis, as a crab flings off his old shell. You are dead, so far as they go. In the Christian world with Christ, your life is a Life all alive with God's Life. With Christ your life is hid with God. Such is his definition of Christianity in the midst of this gorgeous imagery. To think God's thoughts, to be workmen with God, to carry out His plans, to partake His nature, — this is Life as Jesus Christ understands Life, and as Paul presents it to these men.

Except in poetry, we do not speak of God as sitting on a throne, as walking in a garden, or riding on a whirlwind. God is. He is in all space and in all time. Science almost sees Him, does touch the hem of His garment; as in all worlds, in any universe, Science finds Law, one and the same. Faith tries the great experiment of prayer, cries aloud to this Infinite Law, finds that He hears, He loves, He answers. Glad in the great discovery, man studies the infinite purpose of this Law, and enters into His infinite work. Man shows to himself and to all who take note, what Scripture means when it says he is child of God. Man shares God's nature. To make this clear to man when man was afraid of God, was Jesus Christ's endeavor. To persuade man to ally himself to this Living Law and Lord of the Universe is Christ's success. And then man, the child, has no longer a separate wish or purpose. God's wish is his wish. His will is God's will. "Thy will be done, on earth as in heaven," this is his prayer. So is it that in Christian faith man's life, once separate, is separate no longer. In Christ, man's life is hid in God.

> "Father, I bless thy name that I do live,
> And in each motive am made glad with Thee,
> That when a glance is all that I can give,
> It is a Kingdom's wealth if I but see.
> This stately body cannot move save I
> Will to its nobleness my little bring:
> My voice its measured cadence will not try
> Save I with every note consent to sing,—
> I cannot raise my hands to hurt or bless
> But I with my action must conspire
> To show me then how little I possess,
> And yet that little more than I desire.
> May each new act my new allegiance prove,
> Till in thy perfect Love I ever live and move."[1]

---

[1] One of Jones Very's sonnets.

A PERFECT SUNDAY-SCHOOL.

"I have no greater joy than to hear that my children walk in the truth." JOHN III. 4.

ST. JOHN knew they would want to walk in it. But he knew they would not walk in it unless care was taken from the very beginning. His work and the work of every apostle — and the work of him whom they loved to call the Great Teacher — was all work expended, as is the humblest work of the humblest teacher of a Sunday-school, that their children might walk in the truth — from the beginning through.

I do not suppose that I need instil, if I could, more of the spirit which has brought you here into the work of Sunday-school instruction. The circumstances forbid, again, that I should attempt specific advice as to the details of religious instruction in different schools. These must be determined each by itself. I must speak of methods, rather than of motives. But I must speak of methods in general, rather than in detail. I shall attempt to do so, with entire simplicity, in studying not what may be quite possible in any single congregation, but what I should be glad to see made real in all. We will address ourselves to a model Sunday-school, what we wish a Sunday-school might be.

There is no single enterprise in which this church engages, which rivals in importance its Sunday-school. We shall reopen this school a fortnight from to-day for its winter session, and I take this morning, therefore, for some consideration of what a Sunday-school might be, of a model Sunday-school, — I shall hardly stop to ask how far we come up to this ideal, or fail. Those of us who are personally engaged in the matter know pretty well already. And the rest of you had better come and inquire in the detail. My object is rather to show what we can all aim at together, — what is worth trying for, and what is not, — and so I think I shall show what is the transcendent and vital importance of an organization which sometimes gets to be considered quite humdrum and mechanical.

The difficulties in the whole matter are sufficiently obvious. We have more of them, undoubtedly, than the creed-bound sects have. For all they profess to have to do, is to teach certain supposed truths which they prefer to teach in certain fixed words. The process of religious instruction really becomes with them very much a matter of memory. Sunday-school work becomes in proportion much like day-school work. You teach the catechism as you would the multiplication table. When the child has learned it, you examine him, and by the rite of confirmation, or some other rite, give him a sort of diploma. But that is not our idea, — and so this is not our way. Rating intellectual assent to religious systems very low, we wish to instil habits and principles of life. We set the test of religion rather in life and character. We cannot satisfy ourselves with mere memory-work on text-books. This is, by the way, the difference between our theological schools and those of the strict sects — say at Andover or Princeton. Let a man be well trained in Calvin's Institutes and he passes their requisition for a minister. But our requisition is that a man shall be wide awake, and keenly sensitive to every voice of the Present Spirit. Now, it is very hard to organize any school of prophets which shall do that for him. Because all this is so, a Sunday-school with us must be deficient to a certain extent, in that rule and plummet accuracy of plan, with precise tabular returns showing how near the Kingdom of Heaven each child is, and when he may be expected to arrive there, which are so delightful in the eyes of drill-masters, and which seem almost necessary when we speak of a *school* at all. I think it is as well then to confess in the outset that the word *school* is rather unfortunate, and hardly expresses the dominant idea of the system or the wish we are at work upon.

This is so evident, that in many experiments the analogies of a school have been wholly abandoned.

The children have been assembled, not in classes with teachers, but as a congregation for their own religious service. I remember that at Springfield in this State, there was such a service, held in the chapel, at the same time that the parents of the children were engaged in the afternoon service in the church. The afternoon service of the Warren-street chapel — so successful for so many years — was on this plan. I found it in Paris to be the received system of the Protestant churches. It was there organized so definitely that there was a separate clergyman for the children of two or three parishes. He was appointed specially for his gift of dealing with children. Then at their own time the children came together in the church. I was with them at the Oratoire. Their own minister conducted the service with them. They sang, and read with him; he preached, expressly to them. Their service ended, they went home. Their parents then came in and filled the same seats in church again. Another preacher took charge of their service, and carried that through. The children's preacher, as I understood, went to another church, and met another congregation of children there, the service for grown people there being conducted at another hour.

The advantages and disadvantages of this plan are evident at a glance. The instruction given is more fit for the children than that of the ordinary service. But probably it is less so than that of varied classes, each adapting its work to the specific age and ability of the pupils. The chief disadvantage is that the children are definitely separated from their parents in the Sunday religious service. It loses the home character, therefore, which is by far the dearest association that it has. The French system all rests on that worn out notion that the chief growth of religion comes from good teaching. Now, it really comes from affection, sympathy, mutual inspiration. Men know we are his disciples if we love one another. And so here in New England all through the dreary generations when children did not understand one syllable that was said in the pulpit, were not asked to, meant to, nor wanted to, — still because they went to church with their fathers and mothers, and brothers and sisters, and sat on the same seats and sang perhaps from the same book, — and talked or heard as they ran or walked to church and back again, all as one family; — because thus the most solemn religious association was woven in with the family tie, — because Sunday was the one great occasion when all the family was as one, together and seen together: I say, because of all this, the Sunday service, though unintelligible to the infant *mind*, became real and invaluable to the infant *heart and soul*. The house of God, so called, became indeed the Sunday home.

For this reason I do not consider a service specially arranged for children, and taking the place of their parents' service, to be the model Sunday-school.

No! The system which has providentially grown up here in New England seems to offer the most convenient machinery, if we will only give it true life and motive power enough. This is the system of separate classes, each familiarly met by a teacher who is a personal friend, — all meeting together, however, for a united service.

Now, in a perfect Sunday-school, I hold, 1. That this united service — which is, of course, a service of worship, prayer, and song — must be conducted as a very essential and important part of the whole. Do not let us hurry over it, that we may come to the classes. Do not let the children feel that if they are late at the opening service it is no great matter. Do not let them become slovenly in their reading of the responses, or their singing of the hymns. The ease and free talk of the separate classes must have no place in the general service. We are to be as orderly and all is to be as solemn as in the church itself.

The larger part the children themselves take in this service the better. I have been greatly interested in those managements where different classes in succession assumed successive parts of it. But I do not mean to speak in detail.

In general, I have to say, that it is here, and here only, as far as I can see, that our New England congregations are to be trained in ritual; that is, in devout and really kind behavior in church. The New England mind is curiously indifferent in such matters. People's behavior in church is no worse than it is at a funeral, at a wedding, at a caucus, or at the theatre; but it is thoughtless, careless — which is to say it is bad, everywhere where they meet in numbers. A man who comes late to church, for instance, in that single piece of carelessness interferes with the devotion of a thousand people. Carelessness in such a case becomes unkind. Or a person who talks at church does not merely abandon his own worship and put an end to that of the person he speaks to, but disturbs all the persons who have to see him, all who have to hear him. He is not careless merely — he is unkind. Every person who hurries out of church the moment the service is done does it carelessly. He does it because it is the New England habit, — a habit formed in the country, when there were horses tied outside which it was necessary to attend to. But the result of that haste now where it takes place is that the departing congregation look like school-boys glad that their imprisonment is done. Everything of this sort belonging to ritual, in which, in the church, there is great room for improvement, must be attended to in the Sunday-school. The general service of the Sunday-school should therefore be distinguished for its solemnity, earnestness, and order.

To speak of one very important particular: I do not see how we can give too much attention, too much time, let me say too much money, for the musical instruction of the Sunday-school. In the only school where I have ever known this matter to be followed up with what seems to me the true energy, — in the old musical instruction of the Warren-Street Chapel, — the results were a benefit, not only to that school, but to all our churches. I am not satisfied with teaching the children to sing a few hymns well by ear, all of them singing one part, and then all subject to panic if an accustomed leader happened to be absent, or if by accident a child let a hymn-book fall. No; in every large school there must be a considerable number of good voices. I think any church would do well which would take all such voices it could get hold of and give them the very best training the town would afford. I think we should thus in time get what we want, — the same sedulous care given to sacred music which the world now gives to operatic music. The Christian idea, of course, is, that every child shall have every faculty trained to perfection. We will not then have any inglorious Miltons. We will not have any silent and unconscious Miriams. Let us find what we have; let us encourage it, and train it to the best. I see no such ready opportunity for this as is in the machinery of the Sunday-schools.

First of all, then, I consider that in an ideal Sunday-school the general service occupies a very prominent part in the exercise, and is to be prepared for, on all hands, with the greatest accuracy and system.

2. Now we come to the class work. And, first of all, my observation of different schools satisfies me that a great deal is gained by detaching the youngest children in a large group by themselves, in a separate room, with teachers competent to lead little children in singing, in simultaneous responses, and in other such exercises as hold the attention and interest of children of that age. We have never been able fully to carry out this plan in the parish schools, because we have never had exactly the right room for it. But when the Unity School was at Tuckerman Hall we had a most interesting class of more than sixty children, under the direction of a lady of real religious genius and great skill with children, and two or three very competent assistants. I watched it with great interest as one of the great successes of that school. After that general exercise of which I have spoken, these little children are withdrawn into their own class-room. Most of them cannot read well enough to learn lessons from a book. But the teacher can teach them orally what she wishes. They can sing together. They can respond together. They can pray together. And with such a director as I have spoken of, they enjoy the ser-

vice, they "have a good time," which, as I shall show in going on, is one of the essentials of a Sunday-school.

3. Now for the older classes. The first requisite is great personal confidence between scholars and teacher, amounting to attachment, indeed. A new teacher can do very little at first. Let us remember that children of the age of which we now speak have no right to go to the school without some preparation for the exercise. They say they have no time to make it; but that is an excuse. There is not a child in this church but could make time to go to Nahant this week, or to go to the theatre, or to other party of pleasure if he were invited. They can make, if they will, half an hour's time for fit preparation for the half-hour spent with the teacher. On the other hand, the teacher gives more than half an hour for preparation; that is, gives more on the average. Both parties meet, then, in a perfect Sunday-school, with some previous preparation for their exercise. Their conversation must be free, wide-awake, respectful, of course, but perfectly easy and friendly. To gain this freedom is the great victory of the teacher; to enjoy it, is the great privilege of the child.

A friendship based confessedly on religion or an interest in religion, that is what binds together that teacher and that child, — the most precious tie which can come into human life. I will not say which is most blessed by it, teacher or pupil. The boy who, in the hey-day of boyhood, finds in his Sunday-school teacher a friend to whom he will take his questions of conscience, and whose advice he will ask as to his pleasures or duties, has gained the greatest blessing God has to give. And the man who, having passed by his own boyhood, has earned this love and confidence of five or six boys still glorying in theirs, renews his youth, and lives it over again.

It is hard, indeed, to say which profits most by that intimacy. But this cordiality between teacher and pupil is not to be gained without time. It is not to be gained by merely asking for it. I do not see how it can come unless you parents help it along. Fathers and mothers must give such encouragement both to children and teachers as shall knit them together in this kind of intimacy, if fathers and mothers expect that much is going to come out of the Sunday-school.

4. I have already intimated that this is not a school after the fashion of other schools, so that at the end of a year you can tell how far the pupils have advanced. Thus you cannot say that, at the end of one year, the children have learned purity; at the end of the second, peace; at the end of the third, gentleness; at the end of the fourth, that they are so far advanced as to be easy to be entreated; at the fifth and sixth, respectively, they will be full of mercy and good

works; and in two years more, that they can graduate as without partiality and without hypocrisy. True, these are the apostle's stages of a Christian life. But you cannot cut them up in a scholastic system, and inculcate them, piece by piece, as some writers seem to think you can. No! A Christian life is one of those diamonds which does not form itself, does not crystallize, in the operations of an hour a week, in a church vestry, on Sunday morning. A Christian life is crystallizing all the time. Home influence, school influence, street influence, alas! book influence, talk influence, as well as church influence and the influence of the Sunday-school, go to it. And religion, which is the centre and heart of it. Religion, which is the law of Life, is never taught. It is propagated, if you please; it is planted, if you please; it is caught by contagion, if you please; it is lighted as a lamp from a torch, if you please; but it is never taught in words, nor can it be. Religion grows in the child, as he prays at his mother's knee, as he weeps by his sister's coffin, as he loves sister, and mother, and baby brother; as he gives up his own wish to please one of these, or to please God. But it is not taught as a lesson. In a religious family, alive with faith, hope, and love, the child will become religious. Woe to the faithless family, without hope and without love, which wishes that the shipwrecked boy will "get religion," if only as a

A PERFECT SUNDAY-SCHOOL. 53

Sunday morning comes round he may be huddled off to an unknown teacher in some unknown Sunday-school!

Alas for the family! Alas for the child!

But the teacher may help the direction given in the family, as we have seen the family must help the teacher. It is a great thing, where a good habit is forming at home, to have the laws of that habit laid faithfully down in the class at school. It is a great thing, where the hint has been dropped at home, for a doubting child to find at school that this was no caprice of his father, but a little spark from the Eternal Fire. Why, to speak of only one detail in a thousand, aside from these influences of tenderness, friendship, free conversation, personal regard which ought to bind together teacher and pupil, only think how many topics for study there are, wholly passed by in our week-day system, which must be studied in the Sunday-school, if anywhere. Such are all the wonders of creation, so far as God's love is shown in natural history, in insect, flower, bird, fish, beast, star, or sun. Such is all the handwriting of history, so far as His will is shown in it, whether of the Bible nations, or of those we call profane. The very science of morals — and it is a science — is not touched in the schools, lest they should be sectarian. All the geography, history, antiquarian study which illustrate the Bible are left on one side in the same way. Really, if one only looked at these lines of learning, one would see that an hour or two of Sunday must be given to them, as things are, unless these children, when life begins, are to set sail, — I do not say unable to understand their Bibles, but unable to make out any chart at all. I cannot join in the laugh at the old gentleman who, forty years ago, asked a distinguished preacher in what part of the Bible he should find an account of Mahomet; for, really, under the system in which he had been bred, there had been no place in which he should have made any study of what is called religious history at all.

But I admit the Sunday-school has not time to teach much of fact. It does pretend to give suggestion, impulse, love, and life. In proportion as the teachers seek this, resolve for it and pray for it, in proportion as the fathers and mothers seek, resolve and pray for it, the Sunday-school succeeds. Where the quest, the resolution, and the prayer are perfect, there is so far a perfect Sunday-school.

5. But the method of the Sunday-school seems to require that as the children become young men and women, as they enter on the responsibilities of life, all the wider range of discussion, not only on matters of religion, but on matters of theology and moral science, should be open to them in special classes. We call these Bible classes. But that name is very narrow. They should not, I think, be restricted to criticism of the Bible, in which, indeed, they can do very little, but should open on

all the questions of science, of social order, and of domestic life, which come into discussion in any connection with religion.

6. Supposing these various parts in the organization of the Sunday-school, and supposing the principle of effort which I have tried to describe, there are still two controlling objects to be held in mind by the church which establishes such an institution.

First. The Sunday-school is an organic part of the church. The whole school, therefore, is to be steadily engaged in one or more works of charity outside its own organization. It is not to sit contemplating itself. It must be doing good to somebody.

I do not think much good is done in this direction by a penny contribution. It is much better to train the children to do something themselves. Take a girl to some mission sewing-school and let her help in threading needles. Take a class of boys down to see an emigrant ship discharge her passengers, and the next week let them follow up those passengers in Mr. Crosby's hands or in Mr. Hubbard's, so that they shall know what you mean by Children's Mission and Benevolent Fraternity. Those children who saw the "Morning Star" set sail have a great deal better notion of the work of Foreign Missions than have those distant children who only put five cents each into a subscription.

And, as I said before, remember that in all this we are not seeking to crowd these children, nor to force them, nor to divert them from anything which is natural; we are not wrenching them out from any native depravity. We are making easy the growth of what would have been sure to grow of itself. Only, in such a world as this, it might have grown gnarled and crooked.

The idea of force, therefore, which belongs properly enough in other schools, must disappear here, and the presence of the love which undertakes the whole enterprise must be felt everywhere. Or, as I said before, everything is to be done so that, on the whole, the children shall enjoy the school; shall make friends there whom they value; shall feel a mutual pride and pleasure in it, and especially shall enjoy Sunday. How many children, if they told you the truth, would say they hate Sunday! Now this must not be. They can grow up to like Sunday; to look forward to it happily. That they may do so, is, in my judgment, the first distinct office of the Sunday-school.

Such, briefly stated, are the more important points of an institution which may have the highest place in what we are doing for our children. This measure of success evidently depends on everybody's willing coöperation. I hear it said in addresses that if the teachers are good, the school will be good; but you might as well say if the scholars are good the school will be good, or if the fathers and mothers work well for it, the school will work. The truth is, the school needs everybody's vigorous help. It needs the steadfast aid of a set of teachers large enough in number for its very largest requisitions, taking hold of it as a sacred charge, their part of the conversion of the world. It needs their work, not only at the hour of meeting, but in the preparation for it, and in their almost daily intercourse with their childern. Yet this body of teachers must not be regarded as a close corporation whose business it is "to run the school." You who have children to place there have a personal interest in it which ought to be larger than any interest which they can take in it. And I cannot too earnestly ask fathers and mothers, who know what children are, who know what they need, to give their assistance and countenance to the work of the school by taking hold with the teachers and among them. The children will respect this school of ours, just as much as they see the grown people respect it. You yourselves will respect it more and value it more, in proportion as you know it more; and the more steadfastly you take part in it, the more regular you make your own children's attendance, the more careful their preparation which comes largely under your eye, the more vital is the whole. The less is it a mere piece of clattering machinery, the more does it live with the Master's own love and energy and life.

I think if I came here and told you that some one had started an enterprise in North street or at Hilton Head, or in the Cannibal Islands, in which forty or fifty earnest Christian men and women brought together on Sunday three hundred children to teach them what they might of the Bible, of our Lord, and of daily duty, to make Sunday the central day of the week to them, and to carry its influence the week through, to provide carefully the best books for them to read, to interest them in charitable work for other children, and to unite them indeed in a Christian brotherhood, growing up in all the blessed influences of a Christian home,—I think you would give me anything I asked, for the continuance and success of an enterprise so completely in accord with the spirit of Jesus. That is what I describe: only the enterprise is here. The children whom it would help are not outcasts, but your own. And what we ask is not money, but yourselves; that you will lend a hand when you may; that you will join yourselves in an enterprise so noble; that you will help it extend itself as it can, even without bound.

TO GLORIFY GOD.

"Whether then ye eat or drink, or whatever ye do, do all to the glory of God." 1 Cor. x. 31.

THERE is a great contrast between our children's Sunday of a fortnight ago and the children's Sunday of their grandfathers. I am perhaps speaking to some who have joined in the service of two generations ago.

In a genuine Puritan church of the old fashion, whenever the "children's Sunday" came, the children were arranged in files on each side of the central aisle. The minister then left the pulpit, and, as he walked down the aisle, he asked each child a question from the shorter Westminster Catechism. Right and left the boys and girls repeated their answers. There are droll stories told of some unexpected vacancy in the upper part of the lines, from which it followed that the wrong answer was given by some hasty child below, who did not have the question which he expected. Allowing for such lapses in administration and in memory, it is quite certain that every one in New England knew the first question in the catechism, and its answer.

"What is the chief end of man?" is the question; and the answer is, "The chief end of man is to glorify God and enjoy Him forever."

The answer is one almost unintelligible to any child, and is, therefore, rather an unfortunate answer for a catechism intended for the divine training of children. It is, however, an answer which, rightly understood, contains the central and essential truth as to man's life in this world, or in any world. It is especially interesting to New Englanders, because it expresses the real sense of relationship to Almighty God, which was characteristic of the original New Englander. It brought him here, it kept him here, and it made him what he was. In our time we change the phrase. We say, as Goethe says, that a man "accepts the universe;" or we say, as Mr. Emerson says, that he looks upon the universe, and finds that he is a part of it and is governed by its laws; or we say, as Martineau says, that "honor, truth, and justice are not provincialisms of this little world, but are the same in all systems and in all worlds." But in all such phraseology, we imply that man is not as the stones are, he is not as the snails and oysters; nay, he is not as the foxes and the lions, or even the half-reasoning elephant. Man belongs to the universe as one of its masters, who is capable of comprehending its infinite law. This is what is said, in the language of the New Testament, when we read that man is a son of God, is a partaker of the divine nature, or is a fellow-worker with God.

Not because the New Englander said this, but because he believed it, the New Englander worked the miracles which he achieved. He made these deserts, which were deserts indeed, blossom as the rose. He hewed down these mountains, he filled up these valleys, that the car of his God might roll gloriously on. As I said here the other day, whatever he was engaged in, he did it with this sentiment of divine help and of his own divine duty. He split shingles to the glory of God, he shingled his house to the glory of God, he salted codfish and mackerel to the glory of God, he took Louisburg to the glory of God, and he believed he had God's warrant, and that he was in God's service, when he defied King George and the strongest empire of the world. It was because he believed this, that he conquered King George and the strongest empire of the world. It was because he believed he had omnipotent power, that he had omnipotent power. And no statement in the Book of Psalms, as to God's love of a chosen people, and His care for them, was too strong for the old New Englander, as he entered upon his daily duty, as he committed his little state to this or that act of sovereignty, or indeed, in any sense, as he looked forward to a future of infinite requisition.

The daily power which came, either to a soldier, a sailor, or to some man chopping wood, from this consciousness of his own relation to God, was specially nursed in the early habits of everybody who was under Puritan rule. Wood-chopper or farmer, this man began the day with prayer in his family, to this God for whose glory he was going to devote the day. His wife, and his children with him, read some word of this scripture which is so full of the immanent presence of God. I do not say that the passage was specially well chosen for the duty of the day; but, whatever it was, it gave father and mother and child the sense of the existence of the Power above them, — the Power with which, somehow, they were absolutely allied. Whether to break out a snow-drift, or to cut down a tree, or to split a log into shingles, the man went forth to his daily duty with that inspiration. The boy who went to school had not understood the scripture, most likely; he had been uneasy in "prayer-time," very likely; but he did not forget that somehow he was allied to the Power which had bidden the snow fall and the trees grow. I should say that no ecclesiastical order ever succeeded in entwining so closely the sense of God's being with the daily affairs of men and women, as the simple requisition made upon each household by the Puritan system. In Millet's picture, the peasant and his wife drop their heads in prayer as they hear the Angelus sound. But here, where there was no Angelus, where no bell could sound across the meadow, it was well-nigh certain that words of prayer had been spoken, by father's or mother's lips; that the older brother or sister had read something from a scripture which told of God and His power; and, with this omen and inspiration, boy or girl, man or woman, started on the day. And when it was done, with thanksgiving rendered in the same spirit with which help had been asked in the morning, did boy and girl, father and mother, retire to their sleep.

Is anything more simple than to apply this in every day's duty? And is it not clear enough that, if you make a whole city, or a whole nation, start every day with this infinite motive, that city or that nation achieves what we call impossibilities? It is not poetry which says that they have infinite power, or that they are almighty. Without such impulse a man wakes in the morning and goes, languidly enough, to his place of work, hardly knowing what his motive is. Press him, make him look at it, and he says, "Well, I hope that before night I shall have sold more whiskey than I sold yesterday. If I do, more men will go home to their families broken down and cross, more men will be unfitted for to-morrow's duty. But I shall have something more in the bank, and I shall be able to begin next week on a larger scale." This is all,— I, and my success,— and it is not, in the long run, a motive which promises much for your state or for your nation. But, on the other hand, the pioneer of whom I spoke goes out into the bit of woodland where he is at work, alive with an infinite life. "What are you going for?" you ask him; and he says, "I go because God sends me. I go because God has a purpose for this town and land. God sent me and my father and my brother and my wife and my child into this place, because He did not mean it should be a desert. He meant it should be a part of His kingdom. If I can cut down a dozen trees to-day; if I and Nahum and Andrew can draw them to the stream to-morrow, — by the end of the week we will have a bridge built by which the people of the next town can communicate with us and we with them. By the end of the year we will have society on a nobler footing; by the end of ten years, here shall be the most beautiful village in the State; and before I die, men shall bless the energy and heartiness with which those began who founded this town. Thank you, yes; it is a cold day, but I think I can stand it. My hands are chilled, but I can keep them warm. I have devoted this day to the glory of God, and the living God will put me through."

One would like to know who was the author of the phrase in the Westminster Catechism. Of course, if one imagines, as people of feeble imagination did, that God was sitting on an emerald throne outside the seventh sapphire firmament, in a series of concentric spheres like a

Chinese ivory ball; if one supposed that by one ladder, or another, men and women were sending up their offerings to Him, — the picture of man's glorifying God was absurd. Of course, again, if to "enjoy God forever" meant that men and women were to sit round in the seats of a concentric heaven, taking in, from hour to hour, the luxury of such dews of heavenly blessing as might distil upon them in the exercise of Infinite Love, that picture also was absurd. But the quaint words had no such meaning to the mind of the prophet who wrote them in English. Nor had they to the leaders of New England, who took them for better, for worse — for the training of their children. They meant what Paul meant, when he said, in this text, that we are to live to God's glory. And, in speaking of enjoying God forever, they meant what Jesus meant when he spoke of entering into the joy of the Lord, the joy of the absolute and perfect Kingdom of Heaven. "Whether ye eat or drink," Paul says; whatever you do, nothing is too trifling, do it for the greater glory of God, of this Infinite Spirit who is the Law of all Nature, who is the real life of all being. As we ask in the Lord's Prayer that His kingdom may come, and His will be done, on earth as it is in heaven.

To live to God's glory is to advance His purpose. I may know that the deed I do is critical at the moment. Or I may not know this; it may seem to be only one of a million million which put that purpose forward. This is all one. I am to know, all along, that I am with Him and He with me, and that He has chosen that I shall be the creator and director in this particular affair. As I said to the children the other day, He has left the palace unfinished, and now He sets me to put in its place the one jewel which shall finish it. Because I know what He knows, wish what He wishes, hope as He hopes, I go about that office. I live to His glory.

In the critical moments of the Russian campaign, to reinforce the French army on its retreat the conscripts of France were summoned and sent into the field two years before their time. What was called the class of 1814 was summoned in 1813, and the class of 1815 to add to their numbers. These boys without beards came together at the stations, were formed into regiments and battalions, and marched into Germany to cover the retreat. At one of the critical passages of that retreat, about the time of the terrible three days of Leipsic, some thousands of them, with their virgin colors, were massed in a position which commanded an important road. To the astonishment of the Russian commander, his movement, which had seemed so easy, was thwarted and checked and rendered for the time impossible, because, as Napoleon himself said when he described it, those boys and their officers were all so ignorant of war that they did not know enough to surrender.[1]

It is not difficult to imagine and recreate the position. They are beardless boys, — yes; their officers have gone through but half the course of the military academy, — yes. But they can shout "Vive la France! Vive Napoleon!" though their voices have not changed from a boy's treble. And they do. It is the glory of France, and the glory of Napoleon, which brighten the squalid barrack, which cheer the wintry march, which warm the tent or the hut or the bivouac at night. It is for the glory of France, for the glory of Napoleon, that they rally round these captains and this tricolor, as they are massed in the position which an old soldier would call untenable. It is for the glory of France, for the glory of Napoleon, that they die there when the time comes to die. And because they know nothing but the glory of France, and the glory of Napoleon, their sacrifice achieves its purpose.

It is a little illustration, it is a very little illustration; but it does show what we mean when we say a man lives or dies for the glory of

---

[1] In sending these notes to press, I am not able to cite the narrative in full, and I may have mis-stated the place and date. But I think that the story belongs with Ney's request just before the battles of Leipsic. He asked that he might have the young conscripts placed under his charge, and said he would answer for the consequences. "Our gray beards," he said, "know as much of the matter as we do, and boggle at any difficulty; but these brave youths think of nothing but glory."

God. He accepts God's purpose as the critical and important necessity. He does not ask first, shall I be warm, or shall I be well fed, or shall I sleep well to-night, or shall I fare well to-morrow. Beneath this "I" and " me " is the purpose of the universe, the purpose of God. " It is God who gave the command." He says, " It is God who put me on this ground." God's purpose, then, is the first affair. The wind is very sharp, and it cuts my skin. The sleet is very cold, and my hands are stiff. But if this voyage succeed, God's will will be the better done. This voyage shall succeed then, because I am here.

> "I know I looked to wind'ard once;
>   But the skipper smiled and said:
> ' Let no man flinch or give an inch
>   Before his stent is made.
> This is no year for half a fare, for God this year decreed
>   That the forty States their hungry mates
> In all the world should feed.'"

There is the motive, as a fisherman on the Banks lives to the glory of God.

The philosophical historian of the manufactures and commerce of New England comes out from his invaluable survey of her progress in two centuries, with this statement of the secret of our success in government: "Those institutions have their sure foundations, not in ranks or orders of society, not in army, senate, or priesthood, but in the fibre of the people themselves." Our success comes "in the relations of each individual man or woman to the essential principles of society — of order itself." The New Englander's expression of this relation was that he lived to the glory of God. His by-law for a town-meeting is a differential of the Law which moves the universe.

The historian and statesman, Guizot, when he was in exile, asked our ambassador, James Lowell, "How long do you think the American Republic will endure?" "My answer was," Mr. Lowell says, 'So long as the ideas of its founders continue dominant.' Of course I explained that by 'ideas' I meant the traditions of their race in government and morals."

"The traditions of their race in government and morals." Absolutely central in these traditions was the answer of the New England child to his minister when he asked him, "What is the chief end of man?"

"Man's chief end is to glorify God," whether he eat or drink, or whatever he does. The American citizen is to do all in harmony with universal Law. He does all things to God's glory.

CURTIS, WHITTIER, AND LONGFELLOW.

"The Lord hath made all things; and to the godly hath he given wisdom.

"Let us now praise famous men — men renowned for their power, giving counsel by their understanding, leaders of the people by their counsels, wise and eloquent in their instructions: such as found out musical tunes, and recited verses in writing. All these were honored in their generations, and were the glory of their times. There be of them, that have left a name behind them, that their praises might be reported. The people will tell of their wisdom, and the congregation will shew forth their praise."

ECCLESIASTICUS xliii., xliv.

IN the short period since I returned from Europe three lives have closed, of persons not immediately connected with this congregation, but in very close communion with the Unitarian church of America. It is worth more than passing remark, that this Unitarian church of America, not very large in numbers, has been honored by the sympathy and help of three men so widely known and so highly prized through this whole nation. As it happens, I was honored, in a somewhat intimate way, with the friendship, and I believe I may say the confidence, of all three. From the grave of one of them — Samuel Longfellow — I have just returned. And I break what would have been my choice of subjects here as the year begins, to say something of the gifts which have been rendered to America by George William Curtis, John Greenleaf Whittier, and Samuel Longfellow.

I have known Mr. Curtis somewhat intimately for more than forty years. I saw him last, and heard one of his matchless speeches, at Saratoga last September, when he presided at the annual conference of the Unitarian church of America. The president, chosen at the previous meeting of that conference, was Judge Miller, I think the senior member, as he was certainly the leading member, of the Supreme Court of the United States. Judge Miller had died in the interval of two sessions, and Mr. Curtis, as the first vice-president, took his place, and he was chosen his successor. Our Conference is again left without a president, by his death.

His presence on that occasion, the intelligent and thorough sympathy he always showed in our united work, were wholly in accord with the every-day habit of his life. For year after year — at his home on Staten Island — he regularly conducted the public services of the Unitarian church. I think he did not often write sermons, and I am not sure that he often delivered his own sermons. But from his unrivalled knowledge of the literature of the world, he had brought the best he could find in that line to read for the congregation which assembled to meet him. He conducted all the service with seriousness and dignity which made it most attractive. And as the congregation grew larger and larger, with such ministrations of one of its laymen, it always proved, not unnaturally, that they preferred such service to any which could be rendered them by any professional minister.

In the case of Mr. Curtis, this is only an incident, and in comparison not a very important incident, of the moral service which, from boyhood to the time of his death, he was rendering to the community. And this, as we cannot say often enough, without taking public office, without going into what we call administration. I suppose that in General Grant's time he was often, perhaps always, confidentially consulted on important points by leading members of General Grant's cabinet. But he was never in Congress or in the cabinet. He sat with a pen in his hand, and he spoke by that pen to millions who never heard his voice or obeyed his matchless command in oratory. I heard, myself, his great speech at Delmonico's before the Pilgrim Association in 1880. I believe — and I have elsewhere tried to show how — that that one speech saved this country from civil war, in the settlement of the Tilden-Hayes question. Of this matchless power what is to be remembered now, is, that he could not have swayed those men so had he been in the administration. He could not speak as he did — an impartial Minos, looking fairly upon both sides — had he technically belonged to one side.

And again, it is to be observed that the moral weight of the man, his absolute purity, his clear, sheer indifference to self, — purity and indifference known to all men, — raised him to that place in men's esteem. Here was a man to whom it was wise to listen. Here was a man who said what he thought. Here was a man, then, who led and did not follow other men.

Of Mr. Whittier's place in literature I should not think of speaking here. The hold which he has upon the American people is very interesting, — on the whole, it is very satisfactory, — as an index of what the American people are and what they admire. But of his position as a great religious teacher I ought to speak here, and am glad to speak. It is not a little thing that a man has, really unconsciously, written hymns which will be sung for a hundred years in that part of the Church of Christ which sings English songs. I say "unconsciously" has written hymns, for Whittier was, to the end of his days, one of the Society of Friends, who sing no hymns in their public service; and I am not sure that he wrote any of his lyrics with the direct intention of their being used as hymns. He wrote them because he could not help writing them. They express the nearness of God to man and of man to God, as he felt it his life through. Because he was a poet he had to express that, and he expressed it so well that other people took it up and used it. I think I am speaking in the presence of a person to whom he brought the exquisite hymn, "The ocean looketh up to heaven," immediately after it was written. They were all in camp on the seashore; and where you or I would say quietly, " How wonderful ! " or " How beautiful ! " he writes a hymn expressing for centuries that sense of glad reverence which is the ocean's first and last lesson to us all. As I believe I said here the other day, the Hymn to Christianity which we sing so often is an Ode to Democracy which he wrote upon an election-day. How clear it is that, when a man who is in the harness, who is in the fight, if you please, is face to face with other men who think differently or who do differently,— when that man expresses himself in poetry, you have a poem which lives. It is as the old prophecies, because they were written in just such a fashion, have proved themselves immortal, and are read in all languages, from every Bible.

Now what I am to say here, and what ought to be said in every Unitarian pulpit, and ought to be understood through the Unitarian churches of this land, is that the whole religious movement of this leader of our time is alive with the life of our faith, of our theology, of our religion. The Unitarian church is the Church of the Holy Spirit; the Quaker church is the Church of the Holy Spirit. The two are one. We have no reason for existing, — our church has no reason to exist as an organization, — unless we mean to proclaim, " Here is God, God is now," unless we stand for the gospel of the living God to-day. And that is the gospel which George Fox went forth to preach to the founders of the Society of Friends. That is the gospel which he was imprisoned and persecuted for preaching. That is the gospel which the people called Friends brought to America. It is their gospel now, and it is our gospel now. And it is because Whittier sang the songs of that gospel that he is welcomed by the people of this land as the best-known religious poet. For this religion, which we call the liberal religion, is the religion of the American people. It is, for instance, the religion of universal suffrage, the religion of universal education, and the religion in which every man is a king and a priest consecrated and ordained by the living God.

I am speaking in the presence of many ladies who will remember a happy class which we had in the vestry of the old church, when we were all younger than we are to-day. It was a class of young people, who, besides other matters which they read and of which they wrote together, regularly considered the feasts and fasts and other ceremonial days of the Congregational church, to which we have the honor to be born. It was not their business to consider the martyrdom of Charles the First, nor the saint's day of St. Botolph; but it was their business to know what were the religious associations of Forefathers' Day, of Fast

Day and Thanksgiving, of the Day of Independence, of Christmas and Easter, of the discovery of America, and the other great occasions of the Christian year which connect themselves with the annual ritual of a religion of freedom. I used to bid the young ladies of that class bring me a poem, or poems, which should bear upon subjects so large as these in the history of a religious state or of a democratic church. It was then that I first really knew how wide was the range of Whittier's thought and action and song. I have the very curious poetical calendar which those ladies made for the Christian year, and it would be worth editing to-day, as an illustration of his mastery, shall I say, of the gamut of our religious life, so extraordinary was the aptness of the word — likely, indeed, to be an eternal word — which he has spoken on one and another of the most important of our struggles, our defeats, and our victories.

It is easy to pass from such memories to memories which to me involve even closer personal associations. I was honored by Whittier's kind friendship from the year when I was twenty-four years old till he died. Mr. Samuel Longfellow, who died on Monday last, was my daily companion and friend from the time when I was thirteen, for many of the earlier years of life. And when, in after years, we were personally parted more, the old tie was never sundered, and with half the world between us, we loved each other as we always shall. Here is another poet who has furnished to us hymns which will be sung in the English-speaking church when he and every man of our time is really forgotten; because the hymns speak for all time, in language which cannot be forgotten after it has once become familiar. Resisting the temptation to discuss Mr. Samuel Longfellow's writing from the intellectual or from any critical side, I will say that the simplicity and reality of his walk with God appears in these hymns in that natural light, with that single-hearted and simple expression, which of themselves compel sympathy. They lift the hymn wholly above the range of criticism or of any low intellectual analysis. Mr. Longfellow wrote a hymn for my ordination, and I think I should be safe in saying that from that time it was sung at the ordination of every Unitarian minister for forty years — is sung to-day on such occasions, excepting when it gives place to another later hymn of his, written for a similar occasion. He was a man of delicate physical health, so delicate that you wondered that he attempted any professional calling which requires a man to call upon himself regularly for his work, and gives him no opportunity for lying back for refreshment. All the same, in three different ministerial charges, one at Fall River, one at Brooklyn, one at Germantown, Pennsylvania, he illustrated, for the men of my calling, the best way of working under very difficult contingencies. It is no business of to-day or of this hour to say what those contingencies were, or how he met them. It is enough to say that, with the absolute courage of a gay young soldier leading an attack, with absolute unselfishness, which a man hardly understands unless he has seen it in such a life, and with this absolute faith in the presence of God of which I spoke, he worked the miracles of parish life. He brought together the factory workman and the elegant recluse scholar in one and the same determination that God's kingdom should come. It is only a week since I heard the phrase of a self-centred man of affairs, used to his own way and deserving to have it, who said:

"Mr. Longfellow could say anything in that pulpit which he chose. We might not agree with a syllable that he said, we might wish that he was saying something else; but we never thought of anything which you can call antagonism to him, and never thought of limiting in any way his right to say it again and again, as often as he chose."

For me, I have never seen so remarkable an illustration of what Dr. Putnam used to call "the wrath of the lamb," — the strength of a person whose personal life was so tender and modest and gentle that you were half afraid to trust him out of doors, showing itself, when there was any need, in vigor amounting to audacity, and in moral control of every one to whom he had to speak.

He was of a sensitive and analytical nature, which made him detest, as much as St. Peter ever did, anything that was common and unclean. But he, too, had seen the vision, and he knew very well that what God had cleansed he was not to call common. There is not a dainty critic of them all who could go beyond him in pointing out inelegancies. And yet, if you saw him with a dirty gutter-boy of the Cambridge streets, whom he had drawn into the boys' club of an evening, you would see that his was that greatest privilege, the intuitive sympathy and love of untutored children.

Now, here are three Americans — I have a right to say three American leaders — to whose work America looks back with gratitude at the same time, because their death-days came so near each other. They have served America in different ways. But, at bottom, we see that their religious thought, motive, and feeling are absolutely the same. Nay, more than this, it is twined in with the same intellectual convictions, with the same theology. They are three men, absolutely in accord in the moral, spiritual, eternal basis of life. They are three men so absolutely in accord, that, if by good fortune they were thrown together for an evening, in travel, say, or at some great festival, each of them would think that that reunion or communion was one of the happiest events of his life. And this common basis of life, exactly the same for each and all of them, is what we call "liberal religion." Each of them is a definite acknowledged prophet of the Religion of the Holy Spirit.

I have said, I have no right to let such a bit of the history of our time pass without note here. Nobody cares for controversy in the pulpit, least of all for that arrogance which says "My church is better than your church." But, all the same, the truth must be proclaimed, that the religious life which fits an American leader to lead America rests wholly on the simple foundation laid down by Jesus Christ, and rests on nothing else. It is simply the exhibition in life of the two commandments: love God, and love man. And the church or organization which has least of curtain, or smoke, or ritual, veiling that central statement, is the church or organization most fit for a leader of America. This truth is so important that no modesty should hinder its proclamation. It ought to be made in every church in America, when America knows that such men have died.

These three friends of ours had a fourth friend who, as a poet, was greater, I suppose, than either of them: James Russell Lowell. He died a year before Mr. Curtis, with whom he was very closely tied. I am not going to speak of his literary fame or the genius which deserved it. But in the special connection in which I speak, I ought to say, that Lowell also is to be remembered as a great religious poet. It is the poems which express for men man's intimacy with God — by which he will be remembered. Once more, it is wrong that a Christian should not see that each of these poems rests on the broadest and least ecclesiastical positions of liberal or Unitarian religion. And it would be wrong if a Christian did not see that the statements of liberal Christianity were those of Henry Longfellow and of Bryant, who died a few years before Lowell; by which I do not mean simply that all these great poets avoided the technical expressions of the creeds in their writings. It would be unreasonable to ask any poet to put into verse the thirty-nine articles or the Athanasian creed — even if he believed them. But I mean that none of these men did believe such statements; they were all members of Unitarian churches, assisted in Unitarian missions, broke bread at a Unitarian communion table, and wrote Unitarian hymns. I do not choose to have the death of three such leaders pass by without saying that when controversialists of to-day choose to understate the lead and power of the simplest, unecclesiastical Christian gospel, they are bound, before the American people, to say and to show how it is that the two Longfellows, Bryant, Lowell, and Curtis, belonged in form to the Unitarian church, — and that Whittier, so close in touch with the American people, was the poet of the liberal side of the Society of Friends, whose faith and inspiration are identical with that of the Unitarian church of America.

At this moment we cannot think of the poets whom I have named, without remembering Tennyson, whose death recalls so many of the best moments of fifty years and more. Of Tennyson's exquisite life, so happy, such a benediction to his time, the eternal lesson is the most profound lesson of religion. Here again, it is not doctrinal theology, it is no form of outside organization, which cares to repeat the story. Here is the universal, pervasive, omnipotent song of pure and undefiled religion. How exquisite his art was, even the earliest poems showed. But the song he sung for eternity, and the word he spoke to all sorts and conditions of men, were not sung or spoken till he had gone through the fire. Then he sang to us as prophets sing. He had seen the vision, and he told us what he saw. From beginning to the end, vision and prophecy are the song, or the clarion cry of faith, and hope, and love. There is not one word on a lower key. He is simply the poet of true and undefiled religion.

Such lives all teach the eternal lesson. Of the seven I have named all are loved and honored. And not one of the seven is loved or honored because he was learned or skilful. Not one because he fitted word well with word, or rhyme with rhyme; nay, not one because he used well the analogies between visible nature and the secrets of human life, which make up poetry. We love them and honor them because they love, and hope, and believe. They use their knack of language, their learning and their elegance of song, for the wider empire of hope, and love, and faith. They deal with the three eternities and so win their own immortality.

And you and I?

We cannot sing the songs of a nation. Nor can we save it by our oratory. But we can love man. We also love God. We also are immortal. For you and me, as for any Curtis or any Tennyson, there is open a life with God for those around us, in the open majesty of heaven. For that, you and I consecrate life again to-day. For God's companionship in that life we ask him to-day. And it is nothing for us, as for those same heroes of Christendom it is nothing, whether men remember us or no. It is everything that we also walk with God this day, as we go to our other homes; that we also serve men to-morrow, though it be in the humblest services of common life; and that in the dust and smoke of the streets, we know that nothing is common, if we live as these men lived in a Present Heaven.

"'TIS FIFTY YEARS SINCE."

"Say not thou, What is the cause that the former days were better than these? for concerning this thou dost not inquire wisely."

ECCLESIASTES vii, 10.

IT will be fifty years next Saturday, the 12th of November, since I preached in this place the first sermon which I ever preached in Massachusetts. My friends here have been so kind as to respect a wish of mine that I might begin a new half-century of duty in the pulpit under the same auspices with which I began that which is past.

I did not know, nor do I know now, to the invitation of what committee or society I owed the pleasure of standing here fifty years ago. A friend of mine had undertaken to preach here, was prevented, and I took his place, rather unexpectedly. The next day was the State election, and instead of going to Boston in the morning stage, as I had expected to do, I remained here till after the town-meeting was over. I was asked to open the meeting with prayer, and I did so. I was asked to visit one or two of the sick in the town, and I did so. It happened, therefore, that for nearly forty-eight hours I was in Berlin, as it were, as the minister of the town. I heard then, for the first time, anecdotes of the ministry of Dr. Puffer, so long the bishop, under our New England arrangements, of this diocese. I think I may say I made friends in those days whom I have not lost since. For these reasons it is a great pleasure to me that, through your kindness, I am permitted to speak here again to-day.

The two sermons which I delivered on that occasion still exist, somewhat yellow from time. I am not displeased, after fifty years, to find what texts I chose for them. In the morning we considered St. John's direction, " Let us love not in word, neither in tongue, but in deed and in truth ; and hereby know we that we are of the truth." In the afternoon I spoke from the same epistle of St. John, the text, " Perfect love casteth out fear." I am glad, I say, that I know that that Divine Spirit which guides us always, led me, even in boyhood, to choose such themes, shall I say, as the fit starting-place for the duties of the pulpit. That perfect love casts out fear, and that this love must show itself in action and not in word,— this may be said to be a fair foundation for whatever the pulpit has to say or do. As to the way in which I tried to enforce these eternal statements, or to present them to the lives of men and women of the middle of the century, I will say nothing. That is a personal affair. You have forgotten, as, without the manuscripts, I should have forgotten, every such detail; and we will not let any such inquiry into detail turn us away from what are far more attractive subjects of jubilee meditation.

It is no habit of mine to look backward. I have, in what seemed to me fit places, urged on young people and old people, urged on everybody with whom I have to do, the fundamental necessity of looking forward more than we look back. I only ask you now to look back over the course of a half-century, because I am sure that, if we do so wisely, we may get the fit lessons for the half-century which is next to come.

The condition of the country has wholly changed since that time. The condition of the church of Christ has changed more perhaps; and in the hope that from the contrasts of fifty years we may get some lessons for the next half-century, I am going now to look backward more than is my habit. At least we shall find the Providential hand guiding history, for those fifty years which make more than a fortieth part of the time since this text was written. We shall also find that, as a general working rule, the direction to look forward more than we look back is a good one.

It is interesting to see the advance in physical comfort — that is to say, in wealth — in this nation, and probably in all nations. The average wholesale price of flour in Boston, in eight years of which 1842 is the third, was six dollars a barrel. The average price of the same grades yesterday was four dollars.

A barrel of pork cost, fifty years ago, twenty dollars. It cost yesterday, on the average, in the same market thirteen dollars. These figures show with sufficient accuracy the improvement which commerce and invention have brought about in the matter of food, on which matter all other matters of physical comfort follow.

On the other end of the line, one workman in a cotton-mill makes three times as much cloth as he could in 1842. He then worked thirteen or fourteen hours a day, and he now works ten. He is paid per yard almost exactly twice what he was paid then. There is, therefore, either four times as much cloth made and used, or there are three workmen out of four set free to retire from work, to read Dante if you please, or to play the piano.[1] Practically, the arrangements by which they work together are more simple, their promotion is more free. Speaking in general, they have more of the privileges which God gave them when he made them, than they had fifty years ago, as they had more then than they had fifty years before. We cannot too often repeat that the physical advantages of this country were all here the day Columbus landed. But land is nothing, unless there are men and women upon the land. Mines are nothing, unless there are miners. Rivers flow vainly, unless there are boats upon the rivers. The gorge in the mountains is open in vain until men

---
[1] I have these figures from Mr. Edward Atkinson.

have carried through it the road upon which food and what else man needs is to be carried. All this is to say that the world improves in proportion as the men in it improve; while for the rest, the improvement in soil from year to year is scarcely to be noticed by the most delicate alchemy or by the finest microscope. In mines or quarries there is no improvement.

I do not know but I might be fairly asked whether any of the tables of statistics show, or whether daily observation shows, such an improvement in men, women and children as the increase in wealth supposes.

I should reply that this is asking too much. The tree must be judged by its fruits. But I will not pretend that every leaf on that tree is better than every leaf on the tree fifty years ago. This is to be said, however, that the statistics, rightly read, show that there is less crime, that there is less disease, that there is less pauperism, than there was fifty years ago; and that the bitter invective which describes human misery and crime — of which we have to read the outcry every day — really shows a more sensitive conscience, a more watchful examination of the sufferings of men. Thank God that there is this sensitive conscience and this watchful examination!

I do not know a more encouraging book in this direction than Daniel Defoe's "Colonel Jack." It is a description of the position of a poor boy in

London, about the time when William III. ascended the throne of England. The worst pictures in General Booth's descriptions of "Darkest London" do not compare with the pictures which Colonel Jack gives of his own boyhood. And the contrast between that day and this day shows fairly enough the steady advance which has been made in London, even under the terribly depressing conditions of a city which has advanced in population as London has, and which is, as Sallust said of Rome, the cesspool into which sinks all the corruption of the world. In Boston we have somewhat the same contrast, between the pretty little maritime town on its three hills, which sheltered a hundred thousand people fifty years ago, and the crowded manufacturing city of to-day. Yet there the advance is sure.

Now, when we shall come to write history in such fashion as shall show the real motive-power underlying life, it will be a history of the personal lives of men and women; and the motive-power of those lives, say what you please or guess as you choose, is the life of God in man. That is to say, men and women are stronger, if they know God better, and they are weaker when they know him less. They are stronger in proportion as they know each other better; they are weaker in proportion as they are alone. They are strongest when they have the wide horizon, the infinite horizon, — when they live in heaven; and they are weakest when they live in the dark, as in some cellar, with no horizon, and seeing nothing. I know perfectly well that all this statement is regarded as pulpit-talk. It is spoken of as unavailable assets are spoken of. Men say, "You cannot count it, you cannot weigh it, you cannot in any way make estimate of it which will add in with your figures which show the price of pork or of flour." All the same is it true that a community of ten thousand people praying to God every morning, living to God's glory every day, and thanking God every night as they go to bed, is a community more prosperous and strong, a community which has more salt pork and more flour of fine brands, than has a community of ten thousand men and women who, in their daily conversation, send one another to hell five hundred times between sunrise and sunset, who never pray to God, who care nothing for the improvement of the world or for His glory, and whose aim is to buy and drink as much whiskey as is possible. Put it on the mere physical standard: the owner of a street is glad when his tenants are of this God-fearing sort, and he is sorry when he finds that the other kind are squeezing in. Thus simply am I led to what is our chief subject to-day: What, if any, are the moral or spiritual changes which have come in, gradually or by sudden impulse, into the life of New England in the last fifty years?

A new gospel had been preached to the people of New England. The drift that way may be traced, historically, to the period when the independence of the State and the freedom of thought of all her citizens were established.

Where the fathers had droned out in dreary homilies the words which told them that they were children of the devil, and that ninety-nine-hundredths of them were going to hell, a new school of men — Buckminster, both Emersons, Channing, and many others; such men here as Dr. Bancroft and Dr. Puffer — were telling them that they were all children of God, that there was nothing they could not do if they asked God to help them. I remember perfectly that, when I was six years old, or thereabouts, my father and mother took me to the House of Reformation in South Boston, and I saw a body of nice-looking boys, better dressed than the average of my school-mates, going through with the exercises of a sort of Lancastrian school. I heard them sing better than I had ever heard children sing. I have never forgotten the cheerful look on their faces. Naturally, I heard the conversation of my elders about these boys, and the plans that were made for them. Such things were comparatively new, and the real impression seemed to be that these particular boys were to come out all right, as I dare say many of them did; that in the next generation such crime, or fault, or sin as such boys' fathers had committed would be, to a large extent, unknown. There was plenty of money in Boston, as, indeed, there is now — more than people know what to do with. They did know what to do with their money, and they really thought that they could appropriate it in hospitals, in infant schools, in schools of industry such as this I describe, so as to clean up the whole place. These Boston people did not mean to have any Augean stables about it; they did not mean to have any pest-holes at all; any Five Points; any Whitechapel. They meant to have Dr. Channing and Mr. Henry Ware and Mr. Palfrey attend to the morals of the people who came to church, and they meant to have Dr. Tuckerman and Mr. Charles Barnard and Mr. Waterston attend to the morals and the lives of the people who did not go to church.

Simply and absolutely, they meant that every man and woman in Boston should grow up with just the same advantages, social, moral, and intellectual, with which their best men had grown up: say Caleb Strong, Jonathan Phillips, or Josiah Quincy.

In point of fact, this was all as phantasmal as a dream of the Arabian Nights. In point of fact, the people who were to fill up Massachusetts were people of a different education, a different ancestry, a different social order, a different ambition, and a different religion. It would not have been desirable to prevent this. If it had been desirable, it would not have been possible. Indeed, the mere fact of the existence of such a happy valley as they proposed would have brought in upon them from the north and south, and east and west, men, women, and children of all sorts and conditions. As the prophet Isaiah puts it, "The people of the rock would come, the inhabitants of the islands would come, and the villages of Kedar would come." Their dear Boston was to be no happy valley: it was to send out the light that it had, as the rays are reflected from a beacon, to every wormwood valley and every desolate mountain side in the world.

All the same, while the dream lasted, it answered all the purposes of a reality. In those days, if a prophet prophesied, people came to hear with a definite feeling that some new future was possible, — a feeling which I do not think they have now. I mean that in those days if a man announced that he was going to speak on some reform, or if he called a convention to consider it, he was sure that people would come together. But now that call has been made too often. Men have cried, Lo! here, and Lo! there, and there proved to be no Christ. Your prophet may prophesy to-day, or he may call his convention, and no one will come unless he provide some entertainment for them. There must be an orchestra, or a stereoscope, or a collation. I do not say, and I do not think, that this is to be regretted. It is a piece of natural evolution. But it is a good sign of the contrast between those days and these.

Now, what has been gained in these fifty years? To speak first, and very briefly, of visible methods, of palpable things, and of the outside. I spoke of the immense physical advance. That physical advance has reacted to swell the intellectual forces which produced it. Thus there are better schoolhouses, and more; better hospitals, and more; better parks and boulevards and public gardens, and more; better public galleries, and more; better pictures on the walls, and more; and, especially, better books, and more; better libraries, and more. One might spend a course of lectures in showing what are the moral and religious advantages of such an institution as our Public Library, or of the evening-school system in Boston, or of "Harper's Monthly Magazine," or of the "Youth's Companion," or of the Chautauqua Reading Course,— all of which represent absolute additions in the higher training of men and women which have been achieved in the last fifty years.

But these are mere outside signs of the machinery of intellectual force. The reality, that which has eternal interest, is the tide wave of moral force, of which such intellectual methods are like so many drops of white spray. This new force comes in with freedom, as soon as you emancipate mankind. The black man of Carolina is a different man to-day, in every fibre of his being, from what his father was, who crouched and struggled and lied under the lash only thirty years ago. And that is only a little type of the change which comes over every one, — man, woman, and child, — when, as by a miracle, instead of believing that he is born of hell, or trying to, he knows that he is born of heaven. For one century, children and their fathers are taught in their boyhood, and from the altar every week the lesson is repeated, that they are children of wrath and incapable of good. In another century their children and children's children are taught from the same altars that they are children of God, are partakers of His nature, and fellow workmen with Him. History and literature join in the lesson, the songs of childhood, and the appeals of prophets. Every voice and every example proclaim to men that they have an infinite horizon, infinite privilege, infinite duty, and infinite power. New life is in the appeal. It is as when the frozen and hungry columns of Napoleon, who have been stumbling and staggering up through the snows of an Alpine pass, turn the summit at last, see sunny Italy before them, and hear the Marseillaise sounding to beat time for them as they rush down. It is no wonder, indeed, that the united forces of mankind, be they rich or poor, be they quick or stupid, move with a new energy, and achieve what has not been dreamed of, when they eat of such food, when they drink such elixir, when they breathe such air, and when close before them they see the verdure and the beauty of such a future. Your libraries, your parks, your schools, your hospitals, are all, of course, accounted for.

With every invention by which you set an intelligent man to attend a machine, where you had a drudge serving by his muscle, you have changed a slave to a freeman. The man who was shovelling out the manure from the stables of the railway, and is asked one day to fit himself to the care of the electrical machinery which takes the place of the horses, — you have lifted him in the grade of intelligent being by your invention. The man who drilled rock fifty years ago in a stone quarry, sees his son lying on the ground in the same quarry directing twenty steam-drills, which do twenty times as much work as he did, and the son perhaps reads Browning or Epictetus, as the little engine drills for him. You change the very quality of the man. In the fifty years I am reviewing, you have been every year freeing your own laborers as you made them workmen, — men who by the power of spirit used the dead world of which they are masters. Here was a victory of all our region in the nation which more than parallels the emancipation of the blacks, the enlargement of the privileges of the serfs of Russia.

And such a victory is worthless unless the workman knows where his power comes from, and consecrates it to eternal purpose; unless the child of God knows he is child of God, — nay, knows that because he is child of God, he is omnipotent with God's own almightiness. "Shall I drug this body which God gives me for a tool, — drug it or poison it — I who am his son?" "Shall I cheat that stranger, who is overloaded with this care, — or not, — cheat him who is the son of God, engaged in God's affairs?" Send out your boys alive with such a life. Let them know what is a possible Worcester County or a possible Massachusetts; what we mean when we talk of the reign of God, or of the Commonwealth of Christ. Let them for themselves make the picture of homes without contagion, almshouses without vice, village streets without temptation, prisons without prisoners, drudgery of the body changed to honest work for the mind, and of the enjoyment of the best instead of the lowest appetite. Let them for themselves forecast the twentieth century as the beginning of the infinite future. Let them know that they have infinite power with which to bring in this future; and then you shall see the miracles which they can work. One almost says that numbers are nothing; that whether a hundred or a thousand engage in such forward movement, victory is sure. It is as sure as it was to the eleven whom the Saviour commissioned on the mountain, or to the hundred and twenty who left the upper chamber to bring in his kingdom. You are in alliance with the infinite power. It is as when you harness gravitation for one of your earthly affairs, —when the train of coal runs down the incline from the mountain to the valley, because all the attractive power of the whole mass of the earth drives it on its way. It does not need your pushing or pulling, because it is under the infinite control of infinite law.

The work, then, of the century has not been simply the bringing of intellect to bear on the processes which change matter. It is not simply that the brain of a cunning man transforms a bit of pig-iron into the delicate hair-spring which makes my watch my oracle. It goes to a stage vastly higher than this, for which this is only a convenient illustration. In this country, when we made the Constitution, we freed men of all sorts and conditions from every tie of feudalism, from every tradition of artificial authority. We bade every man run for himself, and go as he chose. In that physical emancipation we made the first step. Then, side by side with John Adams and Sam Adams and the rest, who wrought this emancipation, came in such men as Chauncy and Ballou, and Buckminister and Channing, and the others whom I have named, who proclaimed the spiritual emancipation, who broke to pieces those harder fetters which chained men, like Prometheus, to the rock. They slew the vulture, shall I say, which was gnawing at his vitals, and he stood free and erect as the son of God, even as Jesus Christ had said he was eighteen centuries before. It is in the joy of that emancipation that you have the real life of the America of the nineteenth century. It is in proportion as men know that they are not condemned, and cannot be condemned, as they know that they are partners and partakers of the creative, infinite power,— it is in that proportion that they invent more cunningly, that they administer more skilfully, that they lead more courageously. And the blessing came. It has given the freshness and joy which is characteristic of our emigration, of our social order, let me say of our political, and even our commercial, associations. Cynics speak bitterly of the happy-go-lucky habit of our people; it is born from their political freedom, and from the certainty, slowly working its way, that they are heirs of infinite power. For the fifty years which are before you, here is the lesson and the encouragement, that you and yours rely on such infinite strength. You are to harness the everlasting powers to draw your chariots across the causeways you are building. You are to be satisfied with victories no less than those which belong to the omnipotence of the sons and daughters of a present God.

In all the progress which half a century brings about, this beautiful town has fully shared, and more than shared. I was so fortunate, for ten of the best years of that half-century, to live in our dear town of Worcester, so truly the heart of the Commonwealth, so that I knew personally of this and that detail of your prosperity. I knew of the re-birth and of the strength of our own Unitarian church; I knew of the prosperity of the congregation by whose courtesy we assemble in this venerable edifice to-day; I knew when Berlin became one of the musical centres of the Commonwealth; I knew of the establishment there of one and another form of manufacture belonging to that varied industry which is remembered by all true statesmen as being a necessity of a high Christian civilization. Whenever I have heard of the cheerfulness, of the elegance, or of the prosperity of this town, my mind has gone back to the days when it gave so kindly a welcome to a green, inexperienced boy, who had been sent of a sudden to fill an important place which should have been filled by another. All this prosperity of yours is founded, remember, upon freedom. It is the freedom of the sons of God and the daughters of God, which gives us everything we have which is worth having. It is this which changes the drudge into the fellow workman with the Almighty. It is this which makes man also to be a creator. It is when all men are thus truly free, and live in the service which is perfect freedom, that the Kingdom of Heaven comes.

PERSONAL RELIGION.

> Wherewithal shall a young man cleanse his way?
> PSALM cxix. 9.

IT is a very natural demand. It may speak in words or not. But no one whose life is on any system can fail to make it. I am a conscious part of a conscious universe. How shall I, personally, take my share. How shall I do what there is to do? How shall I, if I am to take that old phrase, "Live to God's glory, and enter into his joy"?

I am going to speak in some detail of specific methods in this affair. I am tempted to do so by a letter which I received not long ago from an old parishioner who is now far away. He says, "Our minister preaches to us about sociology, about the improvement of society. But this does not interest me much. What interests me is personal religion." It is some time since I had the letter; but I will confess that it set me to wondering whether I preach too much about sociology, or the improvement of society, about scarlet fever and drainage, about evening schools and associated charities. We must not make any such mistake here. We must not study engines, without knowledge of the expansion of steam, which is the power that drives the engine. We must not have any sermons here which shall not somehow answer the question of this text. Somehow they must all show how God is in man, and man is in God. They must all show "the identity of all spiritual essence and all spiritual life." All of them must show that if man works well, it is because God works in him; that if this century is a better century than the last century, it is because God has had His own way in this century. And if we highly resolve here on any enterprise we will undertake, whether for improving the Sixteenth Ward or for sending missionaries to Japan, it must be because we who are here are born of God and must return to God, because our power is His power, and His power is ours.

To-day, at all events, we will make no mistake. We will try to set in order specific methods by which successful men have made their life divine lives or cleansed their ways. Method is not all, but it is something; and, though I may not mean to wear another man's coat, it may be of use to me to know how and where and of what material it was made. And here I will say, that, as far as reading goes in this business, I have personally gained more from reading the lives of successful men and women, and knowing what their habits were, and how those habits were formed, than I have from any systems or axioms regarding virtue or life. Take this very 119th Psalm. It appears to contain twenty-four answers to this question. In the original, every line of the first answer began with the letter A; every line of the second answer began with the letter B. Now I do not believe that, for practical use, all those answers together can be compared with the value of one of Plutarch's Lives, which gives some real incidents of the struggle of some good man with adversity.

"Wherewithal shall a young man cleanse his way?" or, as we put it, how shall he make his way one of the roadways of Infinite Life? How shall he share in the universe? How shall he walk with God? We will begin when he begins, as he starts in the morning. As matter of practical direction, I should say that he had better predetermine, carefully, and by infinite law and purpose, at what minute of every day he will make that beginning. "I will be as regular in my daily business as the sun is in his, or the moon in hers. I have matters to attend to quite as important as the sun or the moon has, and I will not have them shoved on one side or the other by such accidents as the warmth of the bed, the darkness of the morning, or the laziness of my body." I lay down this law for myself, or God and I lay it down together after due deliberation. But, once made, it is a determination, to be changed only for visible, for real, and for definite cause. Of course, I do not mean to say that it is of any great importance whether a man's coffee be warm or cold when he comes to breakfast. But I do mean to say that it is of the first importance to him to live by law, and not by whim; to live by what is determined, rather than for what is agreeable. And there is no better way for him to enter on such a life, and to place himself in the great company of those who determine, instead of drifting in the company of bubbles and of thistle-seeds, than the making for himself a law, and keeping a law, as to the moment when he will begin the business of working with his God.

You will not suspect me of valuing highly details of ritual. But I will say that he is a fortunate young man, or she a fortunate young woman, who has been so trained — by Milton's Paradise Lost, perhaps, or by some wise father, or by some loving mother — that the first thought of daily life is of habit and of course, the thought of the presence of God. As he pulls up his curtain to see if the sky is gray or rosy, he "practises the presence of God," as Jeremy Taylor's fine phrase has it. It is the present God who shines in the sun, or it is the present God who shapes the snow in crystals, or it is He who determines that the sky shall be gray, or it is He whose spectrum tinges it with gold. "Here we are again, dear Father of mine, — with this day of infinite life before us, in this same dear old world, in which we worked together yesterday and which gave me so much yesterday. I have not to go out alone." God has sent the sun to warm me. He has sent these snow-flakes for my pleasure to-day and for my bread next summer; or He bade the robin sing to me whom I heard just now. This sense of companionship is prayer. To remember that we are together, God and I. Nay, that we are one, I and He; that my purpose to-day is His purpose, and that His object is mine. This in itself is to start cheerful and strong. Given such memory or certainty of one's large relationships and perfect possibilities, and the inconveniences, nay, the discomforts, of life hardly assert themselves. One rates them for what they are worth, which is not much, even at the worst. One starts on life with the omnipotence which of right belongs to him.

"They find they can, because they think they can."

As I said, I do not want to attach much importance to outside details of ritual; but here is a good place to repeat what I quote so often here, — John Weiss's practical instruction. The practical instruction of an idealist, a true spiritualist like him, who ridiculed forms except as they carried spiritual truth, is specially worth remembering. He said, "Take care you are alone every day, somewhere, for five minutes, in which you can listen and see what God has to say to you." I recollect perfectly that either in the sermon in which he said this, which I heard in the First

Church in Portland, in Maine, or in some private conversation, he gave me the almost visible form of a boy in a wholesale grocer's house, going up into the fifth story of a store on Long wharf, and sitting there in the dust and among the cobwebs till he should hear what this Present Spirit who moves worlds, who directs empires, who makes mothers love their children, and babies love their mothers, — what this Holy Spirit has for him also to do this living day. It is this side of prayer, this listening side, this half of prayer, let me say, which is not enough regarded in the wordy and fussy discussions about prayer. People ask how it is possible that this Infinite Spirit should care for a speck like me, and should listen to me. Well, my reply always is: "It is just like Him." But, set that all on one side. You say God cannot hear you, and that therefore you will not speak to Him. That makes no reason why you cannot hear Him. There is every reason why, with conscious determination of your own, you should, in every new day, find what is the set and drift of that infinite river of Life in which you are, and in which you will swim with the current or against it.

The race of men to which we belong is often accused of arrogance. The earlier travellers from Europe in America, a hundred years ago, were annoyed, to the last degree, by the extravagance, as they called it, of the settlers, — as they called people who had been here for a century and a half, — when they described what was to be in America in the future. It is to be observed, in passing, that no man of them prophesied half or a quarter what has happened. What I think important in this habit of prophecy is the certainty that it must have arisen largely from the general sense, at least among the people of New England origin, that they had divine help in the daily business they had in hand. They had not said for more than a century that they were living "to the glory of God," without having the real idea of God's help coming into their daily lives. Now, a man who rises early in the morning, with such habits of life and such high inspiration as I have been trying to describe, does feel that he has an infinite ally. He does not feel as if he were going out only to measure his hundred and sixty pounds of weight against the weight of the world or of the universe. He feels that he, himself an infinite soul, he, the son of an almighty God, is going out to attend to certain affairs which that God has in hand. To such a man "there's no such word as 'fail.'" He looks forward cheerfully and bravely to the day which he has before him.

And here, rather reluctantly, I must leave the detail of the business I have undertaken. I must not try to say how such a man meets his family at breakfast, how he takes the street-car and goes down town to his office or to his workshop. I must not speak of his relations to his clerks or to his masters, to the people under him or the people above him. It must be enough for our purpose now to say that he is not alone; that, in the high companionship which he has invoked, and which he has won, he will go about his business cheerfully, bravely, and with that spirit which, as I said, is sometimes called arrogance by the people who do not understand whence it springs. You cannot make such a man believe that the breaking of a linchpin is going to stop the movement of the world; you cannot make him believe that the failure of delivery of a particular letter is a thing important enough for him to go into a rage about, and make everybody in the concern unhappy. If he feels the presence of God, if he has sought and has found it, by whatever method of communion, he enters upon these affairs of counting-room or workshop from a higher point of view than one does who comes in thinking of "I," and "me," and "mine," and "myself." Dickens's presentation of the two Cheeryble brothers — a real study from life — is a fair enough illustration of the good heart, or the courage which we need not call audacity or arrogance, which belongs to such a man.

I have said already that for my own part I value greatly the biographies of the Cheerybles and other divinely led people who have had to do with the world. And in giving advice to young people I am always begging them not to be satisfied simply by the written biographies, in which you have always to see the life through the stained glass of the creature who wrote the book, whoever he may happen to be. But try to get your biographies at first hand. Try to make yourself acquainted with people whom you find brave, good-natured, and high-toned. Do not go to such a man to say, "I want you to tell me the secret of your life;" but, if he will let you, get into companionship or intimacy with him. Never you fear but the secret of his life will work its way into your life; — and you will certainly find that the man who takes life bravely and successfully is the man who does not choose to look at it as if it were a mere machine of the limited organism which belongs to this body. No; he chooses to look at it as a life swayed by an infinite being, who is in the closest relationship with the Power that works for righteousness, with that Holy Spirit who controls and steadily improves the world.

We occupy ourselves quite as much as is worth while — perhaps rather more than is worth while — with the outside critical discussions as to these four Gospels, — whether the first Gospel was written by Matthew or by another man who had the same name; whether the fourth Gospel were written in the year 96 or in the year 152. I rather think we have got through with the worst of this, and that in the next generation we shall be more ready than men have ever been in the past to take the reality of the message, without asking too many questions about the shape of the letters or the color of the ink. It is not hard to get at the real secret of those four books, and the other books, only too few, which give the secret of the Life of Lives. It makes no difference to you whether there were two blind men at the gate of Jericho or whether there was one, or whether the gate were the north gate or the south gate. You can do very well without distressing yourself as to such detail. If you can get into some such notion of the life of Jesus Christ as we may suppose Paul had, or Lydia at Philippi, or Titus in Crete, or fifty other of these people named in the Bible, who never saw Jesus, whether in Nazareth, in Capernaum, or in Jerusalem, you will be sure to find that, in proportion as that life becomes real to you, does the habit of that life become the habit of yours. You will see what he means when he says, "It is not I who speak." You will see what he means when he says, "Take no thought what ye shall say, for the Father shall tell you what ye shall say." You will see what he means when he says, "The works are not mine, they are the works of the Father who sent me;" what he meant when he said, "Get thee behind me, Satan; thou art an offence unto me." For you will know what this is, — that he went into the mountain to pray, that the disciples knew how close was his questioning and his answering, that they understood the infinite value of his communion with an infinite God. And you will find it easy to give yourself to the flow of the infinite life. These are great words, "to live and move and have our being in our God;" but there is this experience of a few months out of a year or two in Galilee and in Judea, in which we see how a carpenter, who was the son of a carpenter, took on the majesty of life and dignity and omnipotence, because and as he went into the desert to pray, because and as he used infinite forces for the things he had to do. I have never wondered that after-ages worshipped him. They worshipped him, if you please, as men worshipped the meteorite stone which fell from heaven at Ephesus, because to them it was incomprehensible that in these streets of ours, in these highways and by-ways, there should be going and coming one like themselves who was so alive with infinite being. But to you and me this ought not to be incomprehensible. You and I ought to know what the incarnation is of the Infinite Life in a son of man, and how that son of man finds out that he is a son of God. It is for you and me, in the lonely communion of every morning, in the tender gathering of every family, in the cheerful and omnipotent sway of the detail of early life, by commanding the power of an almighty spirit,— it is for you and me to enter into the life of God's sons and daughters.

MODERN IDOLATRY.

THE WORSHIP OF THE BOOK OF DANIEL.

"Thou shalt not make unto thyself any graven image. . . . Thou shalt not bow down unto them, nor worship them."

EXODUS xx. 4, 5.

WE are apt to say that we have come as far as this commandment bids. We may be irreverent, we say, we may be undevout, we may not worship God; but certainly we do not worship idols. Because in this church there is no big stone which fell from heaven for you to hang garlands on, or before which you might burn incense, we feel as if there were no idolatrous worship here.

Still I heard a good address the other day on Modern Idolatry. The speaker, for our condemnation, spoke of men's idolatry of beauty, of their idolatry of novelty, and even of their idolatry of liberty. In each case he meant that people were satisfied with an object of worship and love which is less than God. It is not large as the universe, it is not far-reaching as eternity. So he showed us, and he showed us very well, that our passion for the beautiful, or our passion for novelty, shuts off the infinite life with God, and for God's purpose, of which we are capable, and to which we might aspire.

But idolatry thus spoken of is simply mean worship or false worship. It is not the worship of a thing. Idolatry, as the second commandment speaks of it, is the worship of the work of our own hands, and it is the worship of something physical or material. We say, of course, that it is absurd for man to make for himself a god. The old prophecies are full of satire and contempt for those who bow down before their own handiwork. Indeed, you might ask how can worship, which is a spiritual act, be rendered to matter, which, whatever it is, is handled by spirit, controlled by spirit, moulded by spirit, at its will. Yes, you can say all this, and you do say it with pride and indignation. But all the same, man, the spirit, is housed in a material body. Man, the spirit, uses the forces of a material world, and it does happen, though he be ashamed to own it, that when man, the spirit, has framed and handled matter as he will, either in vanity, or in dulness, or in sheer folly, he sometimes worships the thing which he has made, and the worship of a thing is simple and pure idolatry.

The most familiar illustration — I think it has presented itself already to every one of you — is the miser's idolatry; his miserable worship of physical wealth. It has been forced on this community at this moment by the wretched and worthless life of Mr. Gould, and by his worship of that which is worthless in itself, unless a man shows he knows how to use it. I will say, in passing, that I have read, with a certain horror, what amounts to advice in some of the journals, to young men and young women, to go and do likewise, to lead lives as mean and low as his seems to have been. But I am not going to speak on the worship of wealth, gold and silver, and bonds and railroads. I should say what I am about to say, even if our attention had not been called that way. The worship of wealth is only one illustration among a hundred of the danger which the second commandment points out, and the sin which it condemns. And you and I ought to go much lower down than the study of avarice, or miser-y, or mammon-worship. What we need is that eternal principle which shall save us from mammon-worship, and Baal-worship, and Moloch-worship, and lust-worship, and Bacchus-worship; from the worship of names, and from the worship of books, just as it saved these Jews from the worship of pictures and the worship of images. The danger is in any worship of a thing. I must not let a thing come between me and my God, just as I would not build a room for my library and cut a hole for my window, and then fill that window up with a pane of black marble; just as, on the other hand, I would beg the sunlight to come in, white and unstained in all its glory, just so must I come to God, child with Father, Father with child, with no prison-grating between, with no silk, no wool, nor linen, breast to breast we must come, heart to heart, life to life. There must be no name between; there must be no person between; there must be no book between; there must be no incense between; no image and no thing, else I slide into idolatry.

The Saviour went wholly beneath condemnation of the carver's trade. It is most tender and pathetic, his condemnation, indirect as well as direct, of the more subtle form of idolatry which ruined scribes and Pharisees, nay, half the Jewish nation, in his day. They had no statues of God, no Phidian Jove, no Venus by Praxiteles. So far they had obeyed the letter of the commandment. But still, it was not the Holy Spirit whom they worshipped; it was not the Infinite Being of beings. Like the Samaritans, their leaders worshipped they knew not what. They worshipped a name. This slaughter of oxen and doves, this waving of incense vases and singing of hosannas, was the worship of the word "Jehovah," of the name of God, like what seems and so often is the thoughtless, careless cry of the Mussulmans, "Allah il Allah!" in those same streets to-day. Jesus begs us not to sink into this word-worship. His first appeal to our Father in heaven, to the Holy Spirit, is that He will save us from this word-worship. "Hallowed be Thy name," the first ejaculation of the Lord's prayer, the first promise of him who prays, or his first petition, as you please to call it, is the wish that the name itself of God may not become an image, may not be anything like a stained window, that the word may not be a thing between my God and me. Hallowed means transparent. " That Thy name may be transparent, Oh, my Father! so that in Thine own Holy Spirit Thou shalt come to me, not hindered." And think, or take the book and read, that you may see how carefully, how constantly, he speaks now of Our Father, now of The Spirit, refusing to use the Scripture name " Jehovah," or any other word which might separate Father from child, or child from Father. If he uses any, see how he guards it with persistent care.

Look carefully through any series of conversations in the Gospels, and you will see how the people who were around him, and heard him talk, must have been freed from this danger of addressing their worship to a word. And when, on the other hand, in our day, one sees a congregation of people nodding their heads because the word " Jesus " is read in a service, one understands exactly what he meant when he warned them of the danger of worshipping a name.

But all the warnings of the Saviour and his apostles have, in their turn, been buried under the dust of our idolatries. Eagerly they say, in one word and another, that the letter kills and the spirit gives life. But this is very hard doctrine. It is a great deal easier to pay visible homage to the letter than it is to inspire one's own life with the spirit. And so the world has found it. The same world which is willing to bow the head physically at the name of Jesus, because Paul said, in high rhetoric, that every knee should bow at that name, — this same world, in that mixture of laziness and superstition, has determined to worship the letter of the Bible. That is to say, it has taken a certain book, consisting of the Old Testament and the New Testament, and it has made of this book an idol, exactly as the people at Ephesus took the meteor stone which fell, and built around it the temple of Diana. Ask this same world what this Bible is, and where they found it, and the reply does not justify the homage. The reply is that it is a book made up from thirty-nine books in early Hebrew literature, and twenty-seven books from early Christian literature. Ask who selected them, or who gave them the authority which is claimed for them, and there is no answer. What is very curious is, that no assembly or council of the Christian churches ever came to any agreement on the subject until the Catholic Council of Trent in the year 1545, and that the list which that council made is rejected by that Protestant half of the church which is most persistent in the letter-worship which I am describing. Whoever did select the books, everybody admits that they were men of recent times, who are confessed to have had every sort of human weakness, of whom nobody can pretend that they were specially inspired except as we are all inspired. On this slight foundation the delusion and superstition have grown up which make people worship the words which may be found in those books. Worse than this, when these words are translated into the English language, by other men equally fallible, this same church will go so far as to select one particular translation, and to the English words in that translation pay the same sort of homage. Now this proceeding comes precisely under the head of idolatry. One might say that the types in the Bible Society's office were literally graven images, before which people have determined that they will bow down and worship. The ecclesiastical trials now in progress in Cincinnati and in the city of New York are merely an illustration of a determination of a set of hard men to hold, in visible practice, to the idolatry of the letter in place of the inspiration of the spirit.

If only it were Professor Smith and Professor Briggs who suffered under the devices of such idolaters, I might not think it necessary to speak of such matters here. We should say they were learned men who had taken the chances. If they did not want to take the discipline of the Presbyterian Church, we should say they might step out of the Presbyterian Church. We should say that the Presbyterian Church is a great organism, which might be well compared with one of the great political organisms, such organisms as choose presidents. This is an organization which arrogates to itself also the pretension of a certain divine authority which, so far as I know, no political club in this country has yet done. But I am talking of this matter now because the danger goes a great deal deeper. The Bible itself is dethroned when you handle it as Aaron handled his molten calf, or as the Ephesians handled that meteorite stone. No man, woman, or child will get the glow of the Bible, its warmth, or its light, or its inspiration, who is thus counting the dots on the letter *i*, or the crosses on the letter *t*. In the moment that the Protestant Church, hard-pressed by the spiritualism of its Roman Catholic opponents, descended to the worship of the letter of the Bible, in that moment this book began to lose its real vital hold on the hearts and consciences of men. And when in the place of inspiration you have substituted idolatry, — when the child who came seeking for a mother's kiss meets the hard, unchanging grin of a carved image of stone, — you have, for that child, ruined his Bible.

I do not use language too bitter when I speak of the terror which such idolatry wakes right around us here to-day. In circles into which you and I can go if we choose, to see such things with our own eyes, persons who show good common sense and right conscience in the affairs of life, here in Boston, are at this moment worrying and distressing themselves about the literal interpretation of mysterious prophecies, written, for instance, in the book of Daniel. From these supposed prophecies, they are taught, certain historians and mathematicians have proved that this world is to come to its end within the next twenty years, that the Saviour is to ride into the midst of us in a chariot of fire, that the elect are to be taken to live with God, and the damned to be sunk into torment everlasting. The echo of this delusion meets you every day, if you will open your ears to it.

Now, what is it all founded on? Here is the book of Daniel, written nobody knows by whom, nobody pretends to know. The men who have studied it to most purpose would tell you that it was written several hundred years after the historical events which it professes to describe. In another book, which may be found in the Apocrypha, so called, are certain additions made to the book as it stands in the Old Testament. The separation of the two seems to depend simply on the fact that one of them was written in the Hebrew language and the other is found only in a Greek text. The writer of this book, whoever he is, describes four monarchies, and he prophesies that the Messiah's kingdom shall be the fifth monarchy, of which the establishment was to be very soon. In the eighteen hundred years since Jesus lived and died there have been constantly people turning up who felt sure that this fifth monarchy, or kingdom of the Messiah, was to come in in their own time. One such set of people is now certain that it is going to come about the end of this century.

How is this conclusion wrought out? Does the book of Daniel even say that, at a period corresponding to the year 1895, or to the year 1900, such an event shall come? Nobody pretends that it makes any such statement. But it is said that it makes this and that statement which, when we compare it with modern history, or with the history of the Middle Ages, or with Gibbon's " Decline and Fall," comes out on the results which are proclaimed to-day — proclaimed, very likely, from pulpits at the moment that I am speaking these words. That is to say, I take from the book of Daniel such a text as this: "At the time of the end shall the king of the South push at him, and the king of the North shall come against him like a whirlwind, with chariots and with horsemen and with many ships, and he shall enter into the countries, and shall overthrow and shall pass over; he shall enter also into the glorious land, and many countries shall be overthrown. But these shall escape out of his hand, even Edom and Moab and the chief of the children of Edom. He shall stretch forth his hand also upon the countries, and the land of Egypt shall not escape." (xi. 40–42.) Then for my purpose I prove that this king of the North and this king of the South were such and such persons — Napoleon, perhaps, or Frederick the Great, or Charles the Fifth, or Tamerlane. Observe, I do not get any of these historical facts from this so-called inspired book of Daniel. Nobody pretends that Gibbon's history, or Scott's "Napoleon," or Rollin's "Universal History" were written by the pen of God. But because somebody has said — and nobody knows who said it first — that these words in the book of Daniel were written by the pen of God, I mix them up with the annals which the last eighteen hundred years have been producing. I dip out of my mixture a cupful of what I call prophecy, and then I tell people to prepare themselves to meet the Saviour within a few years, because this writer says, "They that be wise shall shine as the brightness of the firmament, and they that turn many to righteousness as the stars, forever and ever."

Is it possible to conceive of more absolute worship of a thing? Is it possible to conceive a more abject mixture of truth with error, of blackness with whiteness, of light with darkness? And is not here a terrible illustration of the danger that comes upon men when, instead of listening quietly and gently to know what the good God of heaven has to say to them to-day, they choose to bring a book between Him and them, and to inquire, in lost dialects, what He said to somebody who lived in the court of Cyrus? It is against exactly such idolatry that the Saviour warned us, using once and again the very words which Moses himself uses, when he wrote down for all time this text which I have cited from the second commandment.

Oh, if I landed on the coast of Guinea, and found a black man and his wife and children hanging garlands of flowers on some old carved post, where their fathers had worshipped, and theirs and theirs, — where ages on ages had tried to show that man knows he is not all, that there is Higher Power, perhaps Higher Love, — I could at least understand, and certainly I could sympathize. Nay, I think I know how I could talk to those people, and lift their thought from the created thing to the Spirit who creates. Theirs is, at least, a respectable idolatry.

But when it is here; when it is the boy who sat on the bench with me at school; when it is the man who votes for good government at my side; when it is a man who can read and remember and learn and teach; when he comes into my office and talks to me about the four beasts and the ten horns, and thinks that this is Religion, that it has anything to do with worship, I tremble with an awful horror. Really, I cannot reply to him. Religion — it is God with man, and man with God. I listen, and God speaks. I speak, and God listens. It is not the ringing of bells. It is not the bowing of the head or the knee. It is not adding up the dates of the reigns of kings. It is not the looking out words in a dictionary. These are all things. They are untransparent things. They are unhallowed things; I might say damnable things. "Come out from them and be separate," saith the Lord. Religion is to live with God, to move in God, and in God to have your being. He is a spirit, and they that worship Him must worship Him in spirit, as in truth.

TO ENJOY HIM FOREVER.

"Enter thou into the joy of thy lord."
MATT. xxv. 21.

THE exciting dramatic interest of the famous novel of "Monte Cristo" results from the sharp contrast between the introduction of the book and what follows. You meet Monte Cristo first in one of the cells of the Château d'If, a castle-prison which one passes on a rock in the harbor of Marseilles as he goes to Leghorn. You live with Monte Cristo long enough in this cell to know what are the horrors of such lonely imprisonment. And then, as by a miracle, Monte Cristo is free as air; he has what Dumas thought an utterly Aladdin-like fortune in his hands; and the man who, last week, was shut within four walls and had hardly a ray of sunshine, is monarch, one might say, of France, — a monarch, indeed, of the world. He works such wonders as he will; he goes as he chooses, where he chooses; he enters upon the largest life which Dumas, in his extravagance, could conceive.

If you will read rightly those parts of the Acts of the Apostles and the letters of Paul, which show his own personal sense of what his conversion meant, you will find that you have just the same sense of contrast as this in the famous French novel. When Paul rejoices, in that jubilant way of his, about the liberty in which Christ sets him free, he is like Monte Cristo, surrounded by thousands of those whom he had blessed by his wealth, working some of the wonders which seemed like miracles to a writer of the year 1840.

It would seem that Paul had been sent to Jerusalem to school when he was quite young. The critics think he went back to Tarsus, after what we should call his school-days were over, to return to Jerusalem again when he had determined to enter the honorable company of the scribes and Pharisees. Of the intense energy of this young fellow, every church in Europe and America is now the monument. Of his determination to achieve something, — not only his life, but what has followed his life, is in evidence. I do not suppose that, as a school-boy, he felt so much the oppression of formalism or Pharisaism. It is when, as a young man, beginning to think of his own effort, the screw pressed more closely every day, and the fetters seemed more heavy. All very young men are very conservative. Their school themes and compositions are in accord with all which they have read, and they are very desirous of reproducing the old successes. But there comes a time when one finds that the armor his grandfather wore at Agincourt is not big enough for him; and that moment is one of the intense moments of life. To such a one as Paul, there was a distinct prospect of what seemed noble success, when he went up to Jerusalem for what we should now call his theological studies, which was for him the general study of a university. "We will make this Jerusalem to be the Rome of the world. We will show that moral power, and spiritual power, such as are hid in our scriptures, such as are instilled in every office of our ritual, are nobler powers than these of Tiberius, and can in the future sway armies and conquer battles as they did in the days of Pharaoh and Antiochus." With an aim no less, Paul goes to his work, — to be told day by day that he is to inquire into such futilities as the length of the surplice which a choir-boy is to wear, or as to the button of the door which shuts the cupboard in which are the sacred rolls of the law. The first time such an order is given to a young man he does not resent it; he says all is right, and he obeys it, as a cadet at West Point obeys the order which says that his clothes shall lie smoothly upon the shelf of his bedroom. He says that detail is necessary, if you will have completion. But it is when, day after day, the Gamaliel or the Hillel of the college has nothing to tell Paul but this detail or that; it is when one and another new tradition of the elders, claiming to be very old, is brought into the course of study, that the young fellow begins to look more and more grave; that he talks less and less freely with his companions; that his idolatry of his teachers exchanges itself for a grim respect and a hard obedience. For Paul, at length, there came a day when a flash of light swept across him. In one blessed moment he found out that the letter kills and the spirit gives light. In one moment he flung away the armor of Agincourt and the grammar of jots and tittles, and stood forth in the liberty of the Holy Spirit. It was the liberty in which Christ set him free. At the moment he had no more immediate command of his new riches, than Monte Cristo had when he was swimming for his life in the harbor of Marseilles. Bu the swimming is the swimming of a freeman; and from that moment Paul exults in his freedom as only one could exult who had been handcuffed in a prison cell.

In the parable from which I take this text, we are left to imagine a similar emancipation. The faithful servant has been faithful in little things; he has had a little money which he has invested well, and he has made it into more money. But the gist or essence of the parable is the showing how, though the counters be small, the game may be large. Though the things are few, the faith and hope and love by which those things are handled are still the essential and eternal elements,— infinite in every relation of the life of the child of God. To this steward, bred in the simple and humble life of an olive-yard, far away from men, the great lord of the whole estate — the duke, if you please, who sways that whole province — speaks words of equality and friendly courtesy. He has looked over the accounts, and he is perfectly indifferent whether the accounts be in pence, or in pounds, or in millions of pounds. What he sees is the steady advance from step to step; the enlargement which, by faith and hope and love, this honest fellow has wrought, in the little store committed to him. And he says to him, first, "Where you did rule a farm, you shall rule a city. You have been at work upon small things; you shall have the management of large things." But he says much more than this. He says, "From this time forward you are as we are. You are not of those servants who fulfil another's will. You are not of those who must obey this or that precedent of service. You are to enter into the joy of your lord. You are to live this larger life which we, who are lords of the earth, are living. You are to determine your own precedents; you are to lay down your own systems, you are to conduct your own administration; you are to enter into this joy which to freedom, and to freedom only, belongs."

And if you will take the solemn and glad advance by which the pathetic talk of the Last Supper sweeps along, from paragraph to paragraph, you will find that there is the same lesson of the joy of freedom. "Till now I have called you servants; but henceforth I call you friends." The servant obeys this regulation or that regulation; the servant carries out this or that detail as he has been bidden. But the friend enters into the spirit of the work which is intrusted to him. The friends meet together with one heart and one soul, almost indifferent as to the uniform which they are wearing. And of the sacred joy of which the Saviour speaks in that parting discourse, it is clear to see that he meant that those men should understand that in spirit, when he was gone, they were to enjoy this glorious liberty of the sons of God. They enter now, for the first time, into that service which is perfect freedom.

I have cited these four illustrations as the simplest and sharpest way in which I can finish what I was trying to say here a fortnight ago. I reminded you of those mysterious words in the beginning of the Westminster Catechism, as they were laid down two hundred and fifty years ago by the Westminster Assembly. Every child in New England, for nearly two hundred years, was asked on all sacred occasions, "What is the chief end of man?" And every child was taught to reply, "The chief end of man is to glorify God and enjoy Him forever." It is a question hard to answer, whether boy or girl had any very adequate notion what the answer meant; but nothing is more sure than what the men meant who wrote the answer. Of the first half of that answer I spoke the other day. It is the lesson of this second half which is taught in the simple illustrations which I have been citing. The chief end of man is to enjoy God forever. That is the answer of the Catechism. In our fashion of speech, we state it differently. We say that a man must "accept the universe." We say he must live by infinite law. We say that the one eternal word is "right," and that to that word he must conform. But none of these phrases serves us, if it do not include the cheerful, hearty, happy sense of life really complete, of going and coming with infinite satisfaction, of what Lord Houghton calls "the joy of eventful living." This is what Paul means when he says "Rejoice evermore;" and that is what the Saviour means when, to these stewards in the parable, he promises the joy of their lord. The larger life, the infinite life, is not simply the correct movement of a valve, which opens at the right instant because it obeys the pressure of a rod which is driven by a precise law. More than that, above that, and beyond that, it involves the exquisite joy of the bird soaring in the heavens; of the rose at the perfect moment of its beauty; of the baby delighted when her mother returns to the nursery; of the hero who sees the flag flying on the staff from which it had fallen. We are not simply to seek in life a hard-and-fast obedience to regulation; that was the effort of Pharisee and scribe. Rather are we to be sure, because we are the children of God, that we can enter with infinite purpose on infinite achievement, with the gladness of infinite beings. We are not to be satisfied until we enter into the joy of our Lord.

I have been selling across the counter a paper of needles for five cents and a yard of tape for one. I have done my best to see that if I helped the life-work of the woman who bought the needles, or the child who took home the tape, I have entered into wider relations than these of the shop. All the same, I have rejoiced, with joy which seemed to know no end, when my master came in and told me I was to have a fortnight's vacation at the mountains or by the sea, — fourteen days and fourteen nights when I need not once cast up a line of figures; need not once look at a ticket of prices; need not once humor a doubtful customer. I may go into the wilderness and be alone with God. I may see how the pine-trees grow. I may lie in their shade and hear them sing. I may throw a chip into the water, may trace and guide it part way to the infinite sea, and may imagine my own voyage thither and to the ends of the earth. I may lie on the mountain-side all night, and when I wake in the dead silence I may watch the movement of the stars above me, and consider the part which my life plays in the infinite movement of all these worlds.

For my life is all knit in with God's life.

And for this emancipation, for this untrammelled freedom, I need not leave that workshop of my daily duty. I need not mount to the stars to find God, or to enter into His joy. I need not descend to the depths. He is here with me behind the counter. He is here with me as I walk the street. He is with me at this dance, or this dinner-party. He is with me, if I choose to live with Him. So I begin my day with a spoken prayer or a thought of gratitude. I warm my hands at the fire with a thought of the power, the love, the wisdom, and the eternal purpose which makes the fire burn. I go to the breakfast-table to meet the rest, loving them as He loves them, — not for my selfish hunger, but in the common life of united children. I go to the store or to the shop, with the pride of one who creates as God creates — who is necessary that day to the fulfilment of His purpose. I meet the other clerks or workmen as my partners and God's partners. We are in His common work. The men who command me, and those to whom I give orders, — they and I and the good God may be all engaged in the same affair. And that affair is the bringing in His kingdom. Boston is to be a better Boston, the country a better country, the world a better world, because He and I and they are at work together to-day. More briefly, I enter into His joy, or as the Catechism said, "I enjoy Him forever."

People call the sunshine of a life thus spent a matter of temperament. They say it is one person's birthright, and not another's. "Oh! she was born with that happy temperament. I wish I had been; but I never can see things as she sees them." "Never" is a long word. It is a bad word. Are you sure that you have tried? Have you determined highly that you will live in God's world, not man's? Nay, do you know what it is to determine? Do you loyally study God's work in any of its details, — plant, stone, star, tree, child, or man? Do you, day by day, try to trace the power of the Spirit? It is not a week since I heard a man who thought he was discussing the grand politics, skip from guess to guess, from anecdote to anecdote, all unconscious of Him who Is; of Eternal Right; of what must be because God is here. Are not you making that blunder, as you match your ribbons or bleach your laces? Have you highly determined that you will talk to God and listen to what He says — yes, each time when you are puzzled and confounded? Have you, every day of life, made a loyal effort to come at the divine life of this or that child of His? Or, when you meet one and another, do you talk of weather and gossip of outsiders, as if there were no real life, or as if you had sworn to conceal yours behind ten thousand curtains? And have you so set up the body as an idol, — the clothes with which it shall be dressed, the food it shall eat, the wines it shall drink, the house that shall shelter it, and the carriage which shall deliver it at some palace door, — that the poor soul, its born queen, is left in dust and ashes like Cinderella?

Turn from such vanities, as Paul said to the idolaters in Phrygia — turn from them to the living God, His works, His word, His people, His Spirit. These make your life. Live in Him, move in Him, and in Him have your being. Thus is it truly to live to his glory, and to enjoy Him forever. Thus is it to enter into the Joy of your Lord.

TRUTH.

"I must walk to-day, and to-morrow, and the day following."
LUKE xiii. 33.

I MUST. If a man believes he is son of God, he must enter into the service. In this story we have not the full details, to see what is the struggle, and what the adverse temptation. But we can see this: that Jesus is driven out of Galilee by the enthusiastic eagerness of the people. They want to make him king; Herod the tetrarch, on the other hand, would stand for his own authority; Jesus cannot stay there without arrest. He can, as is intimated in one of these books, — he can go to the Gentiles. He can leave behind him Galilee and its enthusiasms, Jerusalem and its petty formalism; there are plenty of nations where he can make himself a home, and live and die. But, no. "I must go to Jerusalem."

He has not taken up this affair of proclaiming God's presence and the possibility of God's reign that he should lay it down because he meets the first adverse gale. Simply, he has given himself to proclaiming this reign or empire of God. Virtually he has said to Herod and all Herod's officers, he has said to all Galilee, and three times he has said at Jerusalem, that all their arrangements and contrivances must give way — human law, custom, tradition, experience, all must give way — before the present rule of the present Spirit of perfect Right. This Spirit will inspire them if they will let him. He is here, the conscious God of the universe is here, ready to teach them, ready to direct them, ready to carry them through. "The kingdom of God is at hand."

Now, to him who has been saying this, in every form of appeal, command, parable, or other implied suggestion, — to him there comes the certainty that, if he continues to say it, he will die; he will be killed; and he has a distinct idea that he will be killed as a malefactor or a rebel is killed; that is, he will be crucified. He can avoid this. He can go into countries where his language is not known, where people are perfectly indifferent to what he says, and there he may drop back into the common life in which one eats and drinks and sleeps, and sleeps and drinks and eats. He can leave God's kingdom to take care of itself. But no. he will not do this. He has received his orders, and will obey his orders. "I must walk to-day, and to-morrow, and the day following."

That devotion of his has given us the word "martyr" as we use it now, and the word "martyrdom." The word in the Greek language meant originally a witness, one who testified to what he had seen. The Christian witnesses, dragged to the stake or cross, did not fail in their allegiance.

They testified to the truth. God is their Father, and they will say so. He speaks to them, and they will listen with allegiance which they give to no others. He directs them to-day and to-morrow, and what he directs they will do. "We will kill you if you do it," says this praetor or that governor. "Kill if you please," is the answer; "that is all one; we must bear this testimony." This testimony they bear, and the word " martyr " has come to mean a witness who is willing to die rather than fail in his testimony.

In the experience of the Saviour, that is a very pathetic and suggestive incident in which at the very close, as he appears before Pilate, the representative of Tiberius, he makes this statement for himself. Tiberius concentrates in his own person the power of the Roman Empire. Tiberius authorizes Pilate to act as his representative in this Jerusalem. These soldiers, who stand at the right and at the left as guards, represent the power of the empire; and to carry out any edict of this governor, these soldiers, every soldier in the empire, would be called upon. Pilate, standing thus, asks this carpenter, who is the son of a carpenter, why he is there; and he says, "I am here to bear witness to the truth." Then Pilate makes the answer which timid men and indifferent men, unspiritual men of whatever type, are so apt to make, "What is truth?" Whether there be any Rock of Ages? Whether there be any divine law? Whether there be any eternal principle of life? This is the question which Pilate cannot answer. But the Saviour puts himself on record of history as holding the banner, around which in all time shall rally those who are willing in the end to die for their testimony. "He that is of the truth heareth my voice."

And of you and me there must be the same testimony. That is what all religion is for, — that men may testify to the Truth. Yes, we are to live by it, and we are to die by it; and any man who will look will find that the dangers of this present day are just what he saw in his time. The danger is that some institution, some fashion, some party-cry, some system of organized social order, shall come in between us and Truth. This is the danger in business, in education, in legislation, and in religion.

And, on the other hand, all success depends, as it always did depend and always will depend, on men's living in the Truth, or speaking in the Truth. I send an expert into my mine to tell me how wide is my vein of silver. He must tell me the truth. He must not tell me what he hopes or wishes or believes. I read the record of the weather in the newspaper. Fifty observers all over the country must tell me the truth. They must not guess at the temperature; they must look at the thermometer. Or I am buying and selling. Cotton, wool, flour, grain, sugar, coffee, tea, spice, coal, wood, or whatever it may be, I want to know the truth about the stock in the market, the stock to arrive, the price yesterday, and the price a year ago. Indeed, if we sift it down, the reason why this century does things better than the darkest century of the Dark Ages, is that this century finds it easier to come at the truth. Never were men more eager to set this world forward than Thomas Aquinas, or Roger Bacon, or hundreds of those men who sat in darkness. But when they sought for the truth, they could not find it in a thousand works and ways where we can find it and do find it and have it in our hands. Thus, I know which way the wind blew at San Francisco last night. I know, if I choose, what was the revenue of the government last week or last year. With my duty to perform to-morrow and my path to choose, I step forward in a world which, after a fashion, is finding out that there is little good in secrecy, and no good in lying; has found out, on the whole, that it is wise and well to discover and to proclaim the truth.

This true allegiance of man to the Infinite Law implies and involves more than verbal truth. It is the obedience of every act, so that the man does without concealment, without pretence, without exaggeration, the thing he undertakes to do. The errand boy does not loiter on his errand. The sentinel never misses a turn of his round. The screw-maker never puts one deficient screw in the parcel. We shall gain this absolute allegiance when the kingdom of God wholly comes. To gain it, to bring in that kingdom, is our present hope and duty. In our own time all the plans of religious men looking toward this aim are helped forward and confirmed by the steady determination of the men who study Nature and extort her secrets. The pretences of men of science are ended. They study the Truth wherever it may lead them. The theory must go if the obdurate fact will not sustain it. To note the fact, that is, the thing which has been made, and by loyal comparison of a hundred facts to work out the truth which unites and comprehends them all, this is the business of the men of physical science. When he only tells you of things, he tires you and annoys you. But when he rises to the truth behind the thing, he gives you courage and makes your life larger. Now, it is in this accuracy of observation, and in its stern veracity of report, that the science of to-day becomes a part of the religion of to-day, and that both of them, Science and Religion, really hold up each other's hands. To know the reality which is, and to stand by it, to live for it, and, if need be, to die for it, — this is the watchword. This it is to be of the Truth; to be a seeker of the Truth. Whoever enters on this noble enterprise leads mankind by so much forward. He becomes also one of the leaders; he is one of the benefactors of his kind. Easy for him to see how Jesus Christ, who lived for this Truth, testified to it, and died for it, became by that life and death the Saviour of mankind. Easy to comprehend what that Saviour meant when he said, "The Spirit of Truth shall come to you, and he shall lead you into all truth."

Because it was the Truth he proclaimed the reign of God. The "glad tidings" of the reign of God they called it; and well they might. God as ruler, instead of this adulterous Herod or this arbitrary Pilate. God's law, simple and certain as sunrise or as the cooling dew, in place of this tithing of weeds, this ringing of bells, this sacrifice of oxen, this jot and that tittle of formality. God here, in me, in you, instead of God on His sapphire throne yonder in the highest heaven, instead of God in the Holy of Holies. Glad tidings is all this, indeed, if only any one can really believe and take it in; if one can live as the companion of such a father, can speak His word and do His will. If one can do it with as little jar and protest as the stars yonder move in heaven. Jesus, who proclaims it now, has from a boy received it. Obedient to his mother, in the joy of home, he has lived in favor with God and man. But when he went to Jordan, yonder, he saw that the time had come for more than home joys, more than the daily duty with his tools. The time is ripe. All men in this world must know — they must be forced to know — that the dear Father of us all has not forgotten us. We are here because He is here. We think because He knows. We see because He sees. We live because He lives. Let us listen; He is speaking. Let us speak; He will hear us. We can tell Him everything: of our daily needs, — " food for to-day's life, dear Father;" of our temptations and trials, —" forgive us, dear Father, and deliver us from evil." To show to all around him — to Peter and Andrew, to Mary and Salome — that he knows that this is so; he must speak to them and theirs. That a larger circle may see it and know it than this of village friends. He must send others to tell it, and they must send others all round the world.

From century to century since, different generations of men have honored him, in a way have loved him. They could not help that. He compels men's love even though they read it only in these fragments of history. But as to this reign of God, it seems as if men hated to receive anything so simple. An unseen Spirit, whose voice does not make air vibrate, here in this workshop, between me and my fellow-workman, that cannot be what he means by God's reign! And so such a church as that at Rome proposes a human monarch who shall be the spiritual Father of the world. And he and his council shall direct a thousand bishops — overseers of mankind; and they shall direct each his hundred or his thousand priests. See, there a kingdom worth talking of! Or, on quite another side, catching up the gorgeous poetry with which he describes the fall of the temples of hell and the glorious coming of God, another set of word-worshippers fix the day and the hour when a procession of cherubim and seraphim, angels and archangels, with names and without them, with trumpets and with cornets, shall come marching or flying into the world, and from some central city or empire shall set right what is wrong. All which is but the continuance of the idolatry, the worship of a Form, of which he was so tired. Yet the best men sometimes show a longing for it. Mr. Seeley, who certainly apprehends the dignity and purity of the Saviour, does not look out on the infinite horizon, of what the Saviour proposes. He tells us that the kingdom of God is to be a society of those who join hands and confederate. He calls it a club. It is a self-elected company out of the millions of mankind. But this is not so. With the Saviour it is no pageant to be applauded; it is no hierarchy to be catalogued; it is no thing to be looked upon and with brush or words described. Simply, it is the reign of God.

God here and God now has come, and my work is done in the school-room. Oh, no, not quite done! Here is this tired boy; he has been lazy, if you please; he cannot understand his sum. Will I please stop and show him? How easy to tell him to work it out himself! How easy to show him that his dulness is his own fault! How pleasant to stretch off for my hour's walk over the fields yonder! Yet I must not check him thus. I must stay. This is God's school-room. Here is God's empire. He reigns here. His kingdom is at hand,

Or these treenails we are driving in the ship are but poor stuff. They must have rotted somewhere. If I condemn them, if I ride over to the village, I can get some which are not shaky, which will stand the strain. True, I shall be abused by the boss. He will say I am wasting time and money. I cannot help that. I must not spoil his ship for him. Indeed, it is not his ship as much as it is God's ship. God reigns in this ship-yard. His Kingdom is at hand.

Or I am a member of the French Parliament. Here are the unpaid bills for my family expenses. The doctor is not paid who cared for my boy when he was burned so badly. I cannot send his brothers to school for lack of money, and here comes by mail a check for 25,000 francs, and a request that I will speak for the Panama loan this afternoon. I was all ready to speak for it. Here is the speech on my desk. But I must not take the money, — must not. This is God's chamber. His reign is at hand.

Or I am an American citizen in my little shrine on the day of the election. Here is George's name, which I may vote for or against. George does not like me. He has often abused me. He prejudiced the bank directors against me. He pointed me out for the scorn of the whole company one day. But it happens that he stands on this ticket for good government, for law and order, for purity instead of drunkenness, for peace instead of war. I must vote for George though he has been unjust to me. For this is God's polling-booth and His temple. We are in His empire. His kingdom is at hand.

Every one of us may, when he chooses, enter on this business and proclaim this news, for news it is: That God is here, and is on our side. And life will grow simple as He does. For all duty will cluster round this one motive. As it grows simple it will grow serene, and gentle, and easy to be entreated. And it will grow strong. How can I be weak if all Nature is on my side, if God seconds or leads all I have to do? And life grows more glad, for it is more harmonious, when there is no jar nor discord, when my song rings in exact accord with this great diapason of the universe.

Simplicity, serenity, strength, joy, and harmony, these are what I gain when I make the Truth my only counsellor; when I know I must say what Truth bids me. Even if the Truth compel me to persevere to the end. If I loyally obey the voice, I must walk as Truth directs me.

HOW TO USE THE BIBLE.

"The letter killeth, but the spirit giveth life."
2 Cor. iii. 6.

I HAVE no right nor wish to say what I said of Bible worship last week without saying more. I tried to show, even bitterly, as perhaps you thought, that we must not make an idol of it — a fetich — as if it were a stone which fell from heaven. I must not say this without showing what we can do with it, and what it can do for us.

The Bible has certainly been the greatest religious educator of the modern world. In a volume, not large, have been songs, lessons, histories, which have made men live. Those nations which have read the Bible most have lived the most. That is a clear bit of history. Now, how are we to keep the life, while we refuse to be chained by the idolatry?

We are to do just as we do with all other lessons and achievements of the men of past times. We keep the lesson, and we set aside the method; we accept the spirit, and we reject the letter; we live the life, and are careless about its machinery.

This needs no elaborate statement. Take a

simple, every-day fact. Soon after white men had
settled here, they found that they needed a road
from Boston to New York. How did they make
it? Did any surveyor draw a straight line on
the map from one village to the other, and then
push a road over the mountains, and across the
swamps and rivers? Not at all. That is not the
order of society or history, any more than it is
the order of physical nature. The first traveller
by land followed the trails, as they were still
called, which Narragansetts, Mohegans, and Pe-
quods had made. That is, after he left Providence, he kept nearly, though not quite, parallel
with the seaboard. The Indian path had to keep
on the land-side of the bays and other inlets, but
it had to keep on the water-side of the hills and
forests. Then, on the line of this rough Indian en-
gineering was eventually built the white man's road.
In Rhode Island, they call it Queen Anne's road,
because it finally took decent form in her day.
This is very well for a beginning.

But time goes on. The whole country is
settled. Dark forests give way to sunlight and
air. Time becomes more precious as civilization
advances. One of you wants to see his partner
in New York, yet you must be here in your
counting-room every day. Six hours even seems
too long a time for the journey in either direction.
You take the railroad men to task if they exact
six hours. You say, "I must go in five hours.

I ought to go in four. You must straighten this curve, you must cut off that corner."

Now, suppose a great corporation of these railroad men replied, "This is out of the question. You are defying God. You are changing the whole record of His will. He determined that people should go by that old road. If He had not so determined, the Indians would not have travelled there. Roger Williams and John Mason would not have gone there. And see here; here is a letter from Benjamin Franklin in which he says that this is an excellent road, and that the mail of the colonies shall march over it. And here is a letter from General Greene in which he says that the Army Corps found it a very quick road when they marched to New York, in 1776. Do you pretend that you are wiser than Benjamin Franklin? Do you say you know more of moving armies than Nathaniel Greene?"

If a strong corporation of railroad men took this ground, they would take exactly the ground which the Synod of the Presbyterian Church of New York now takes in trying Dr. Briggs for heresy, and which the Synod in Ohio takes in condemning Dr. Smith for heresy. Their argument, if you strip off all entanglements, is this: Since the invention of printing, particularly since the translation of the Bible into the daily language of common people, it has been the most important single means of quickening the life of men who have used it. It has done more than any other agency to bring man and God together, and to lift men into a divine life. Therefore, no one shall say that there are any human errors in this divine book; no one shall point out such errors; and every one shall say that one part of it is as valuable as another. In practice, this comes out in saying that the Bible is the only important instrument for bringing men and God together. It comes out on such idol worship as I spoke of last week, when I described the idolatry which worshipped the Book of Daniel.

Now, we will not be satisfied with protest against idolatry. How can we truly and well use the Bible? That is our real question. Look forward and not backward. That is our direction. The man who lives in the Spirit, who wants to commune with God, and to enter into His life, how far does this person use the Bible? how far does he use every method which the past puts into his hands? How far does he accept the prophets and seers of the past as his leaders, and at what point does there come in the inspiration or the instruction of the thousand seers and prophets who are speaking to-day of God, and heaven, and duty? How are the two to be blended, the power of the past and the power of the present? Where does one begin and where does the other end? These are great questions. In a certain sense, you might say that it takes all life to answer them. Still, in a fashion, the greatest question can be answered in three words. And in a community trained like ours, I have no right to leave what I said last Sunday without making some answer to these questions now.

The Bible, then, is a record, as good as those men could make, of what certain prophets and seers have found out about God and His ways with men. Sometimes they have stated this well, sometimes not so well, and sometimes badly, as when David expresses the wish that the heads of those little children should be dashed against the stones. But on the whole, it is a record, now historical, now poetical, and now didactic in intention, of God's intimacy with man, and man's intimacy with God. Because it is, these forty or fifty little books in it have preserved themselves, or been preserved, while thousands of books which seemed of more importance have been lost, or have been wholly forgotten. Because of this intercommunion of God and man, because of this truth here illustrated, that man can speak to God and can hear God, that God can speak to man and will hear man, this book exists. It lies on this desk, it is in your homes, because it sets out this intimacy so closely. To any person, then, who has any reverence for the Bible, any regard for it, or any gratitude, the Bible speaks itself constantly to say, "For the very love of God, of the God of whom you read in this book, seek Him yourself, and

HOW TO USE THE BIBLE. 153

listen to Him yourself." Listen as Amos listened when he was herding cattle in Tekoa. Listen as Habakkuk listened as he stood a sentinel upon the tower. He watched to see what God would say to him. He watched to see what he should say when he was reproved. And you and I? We are not sentinels on towers perhaps, we are not herding cattle perhaps, but we are somewhere, and we are in God's service. We are children of God and partakers of His nature, if we choose. And we are to listen for His words as these prophets listened. We are to proclaim what He has said to us as they proclaimed. As they begged Him to enlighten them, we are to beg Him. As they thanked Him gratefully, we are to thank Him. As they rejoiced in His answer, we may rejoice. As they looked forward to better times, we may look forward. I say, we may; but we shall not, unless we seek. We shall not hear unless we listen. We shall not see if we shut our eyes. No word of God says or implies that we are His so entirely that His life shall flow into ours, unless we seek that blessing. Every promise, whether the promise of spring-time, the promise of poetry, or the promise of experience, may be stated as the promise of Scripture is stated, that it is those who ask that shall receive; those who look that shall discover; those who knock to whom it shall be opened. "If ye seek me, surely ye shall find me, if ye seek for me with all your heart." This is the promise of Scripture, and it is avouched through and through in the voices of out-door nature and of human experience. And simply, this is to say, that every man who reverences the Bible, who loves the words and the promises of the hundred children of God who speak to Him in this Bible, is bound by that love and reverence to join himself to their number, to listen every day to the present word of the Holy Spirit, and every day to proclaim that blessing to those who are around him.

And how shall he listen? How shall he prophesy? Listen as these men listened. They did not sit down with a pile of books about them, with a multiplication board and slate and pencil, to demonstrate by the mathematics the being and attributes of God. They sought Him where they were, and where they were they found Him. Habakkuk on his watch-tower, Hosea as he was riding after those cattle, Isaiah as he led a party of pioneers, and set this squad with their pickaxes to hew down a hill, and that squad with their harrows to fill up a morass. In the open air, I observe, most of them sought Him and found Him. But there is no place where I may not seek Him, and no prison where I may not find Him. Only this is to be said, that when I am under the open heaven, when I am on the shore of His boundless sea, when I am alone in what seems His endless forest, when no prattle of man interrupts His whisper, when no dust from man's digging obstructs the vision, it does seem more certain that I hear that simple word of loving wisdom, or that I comprehend the majestic miracle of absolute power. Thus is it that the woods are always God's temple; the sky is always His vaulted arch, and the ocean is always a fellow-worshipper. Thus is it that on the field of my microscope I see God creating now, and I enter into His life, I comprehend something of His motive, I sympathize with His will, so far as I can conceive it. Thus I know and feel that I am His and He is mine. I love because He loves. I move with His power. I live in His life. In proportion as I enter into the present life of His unspoiled and untarnished world, in that proportion am I sure that He is Father and that I am child.

It is not that a man is to be kind to his wife because some oracle says so, or kiss his child because a text has directed it. There is no such magic in text or oracle. That sort of obedience makes the law as dreadful as it was to Paul. You cannot compel Life by your statutes. But you can inspire it by your Bibles. It is because the Spirit gives life by the same certainty in which the letter kills it, that this Bible has inspired the modern world. To enter into the spirit of Paul, — reconciling the contentions in these little societies, — that is possible to him who reads. To make the life of the Saviour as real as is the life of your brother who is travelling in Norway, of your daughter who is at school at Wellesley, this is in your power if you choose. True, you may measure out a dose of Bible for the morning and another for the evening, and five for Sunday, to be "taken" as if by the quack direction on some bottle of medicine. But you may enjoy with your Saviour the open air of Galilee; you may wonder with his wonder and grieve with his sorrow, as this man asks you for a sign, or as that one wants to divide an inheritance. You may enter into the Life of lives, and bid the letter go. You may leave Galilee with him and shun the dangerous multitudes. You may walk to Jerusalem with him, as other disciples did, with better understanding than they had of the mood in which he travelled. You may stand by in sympathy when Pilate sat in judgment. You may follow in tears as men lead him along the Way of Sorrow. You may enter into his spirit; and in that spirit you may pace your way of sorrow; you may take your journeys; you may join your multitudes or leave them; you may enjoy your sunshine. And such gift of life you will take, if you scorn the letter which kills, and with all the glow of imagination, all the sympathy of love, and all the right to interpret, which any child of God has when he reads or thinks of the Son of God, who has led the world, if you make your Bible your friend, and will not let it be your tyrant. Such gift and privilege are given to the prophets of the Most High, to the sons and daughters of the living God.

We are here to live, — to live more to-day than yesterday. To work? Yes, so far as work helps life. To play? Yes, so far, and no farther. To be alone? If solitude helps life. To be together? If society helps it. So is it certain that the record of the past, of its prophets and martyrs, its poets, and its Saviour, shall quicken life for us, if we read in the Spirit, if we live in the Spirit, if we speak in the Spirit. Death unto death is that bondage of the letter. But the work of the Spirit is joy, and peace, and love, and life.

Nor will any one sink into a selfish worship, or into self-worship, who rightly takes in the spirit of the Bible. Notice how it deals with multitudes or nations, and in the end with the whole world. "Thy kingdom come, thy will be done in the whole earth as it is by the moving stars." In the very beginning you have the blessing of families, and then of the whole race of Ishmael and Isaac, Abraham's children. It is then the march of a nation from Egypt, and it is the history of a nation which you follow. If you turn aside to a bit of personal biography, like that of David, still David is singing for you the psalms of a whole world. You cannot get, even from the simplest idylls of the Old Testament, or from the little bits of family tradition,—you cannot get the introspection in which a man makes himself all alone, or fights his battle regardless of the battles of other men. As you come later down, as there lie open even wider horizons, you find Isaiah and the prophets rebuking Israel for thinking that Israel was alone or could be alone. And, of the New Testament, the whole Spirit is the Spirit which brought on the Master the prosecution of the Nazarenes, when he told them to their faces that God had shown his choicest favors to Syrian and Gentile. From family to tribe, from tribe to race, from Hebrew to Gentile, and from both to the whole world of man, the Bible leads us up step by step. And, as I say, whoever takes in its spirit, begins, at least, to understand what are the ties which link him with the race; or, better, what is the common life which beats in the hearts of all men. It is not simply an outside duty by which I bear my brother's burden; it becomes a necessity of my being. The hand cannot say to the foot, I have no need of thee. Our joy is one joy, our sorrow is one sorrow, our destiny is one destiny. And I do not read my Bible to any purpose, unless I find that such is its inspiration. Here, then, is another of its lessons for my life to-day. If fashion have separated me from my fellows, if vanity or pride have separated me, if shyness have separated me, which is said to be the constitutional weakness of the great race to which we belong,—if, for any cause, I have gnawed my own heart or counted my own sins or sought a lonely by-track of salvation, my Bible ought to drag me out from such loneliness, and compel me to live in the common life. Am I indeed a prophet of the living God, as the Bible says I am? Then I am a prophet who am to proclaim to all the world, to every creature in it, if I can, the good tidings with which the Bible culminates. This is indeed the Saviour's last spoken word, and this is the great direction of the Bible.

It compels my intimacy with others. You say you had rather live alone? So some honey-bee says he had rather live alone; he tries the experiment, and you find him dead on the outside of the hive. Your life is a common life, and you can no more live alone, than a cell beneath the bark of an elm-tree can live alone. Give and take, lend and borrow, is the law of the being of the cell, it is the law of the bee's being, and it is your law and mine. Every such word as conversation, communion, intercourse, comfort, sympathy, — anything which brings in the interplay of life, helps to illustrate what I will not call the duty, but the privilege, or, if you please, the necessity, which is upon each and all of us, if we are to live as sons and daughters of God. Here it is that all real literature which belongs to the history of our race is a help to us. Here is it that every form of society, however it seems to fail, and indeed does fail, has, because it is society, its advantage. The high society which books give becomes a reality in our infinite training. If I know Mary Ware, if

I know Florence Nightingale, if I know Oliver Cromwell or Martin Luther, if I know Saint Francis of Sales, if I know Clement of Alexandria, if I know Paul of Tarsus, if I know Jesus of Nazareth, I am the larger man for the knowing. And I do not read my Bible to any purpose unless I find this out.

"WALK IN THE SPIRIT." These are the words in which Paul sums up Christian duty. Read in the Spirit; these give the lesson for Bible-reading. And he who refuses to worship the letter, ought, all the more certainly, to learn that The Spirit gives Life.

THE LIGHT OF THE WORLD.

"Neither do men light a lamp, and put it under the bushel, but on the stand; and it shineth unto all that are in the house."
MATTHEW v. 15.

THE democracy of the four Gospels is the terror of most established churches, as it is the great marvel of history.

Take this phrase, certainly central, in the Sermon on the Mount, — "The light of the world."

Here is the fulfilment of prophecy, — " The people who sat in darkness have seen a great light." And there can be no nobler phrase to describe the history of what "transpired" eighteen hundred and sixty years ago, than to say that, in a world dark as death, the light appeared. You cannot help seeing that light appeared. Sceptic or credulous, you have to agree, at that point in history, that then and there light appeared. Nay, there is one moment and one place when a certain dignified and impressive announcement was made of the principles on which the new reign of things was to move forward. On a mountain-side, which they will show you to-day if you will go there, in a recess in the slope, which the geologists say is the crater of a dead volcano, — dead, as for the lesson of light and life it should be, — there has gathered a great company of people from all Syria, from all the east of the Mediterranean. To them the Teacher speaks who is to unfold the new lesson. Now we shall know what the light of the world is.

And he says, — if you think he knows, you must believe, — he says to camel-drivers from Damascus, to shepherds from Edom, to fishermen from Bethsaida, to vine-dressers and olive-men from Cana, — he says to publicans and sinners who have come to hear him, — to this great multitude he says, "Ye are the light of the world."

It is no wonder that such radical appeal to the multitude is the terror of the establishments of priests. It is no wonder that the Gospel of Matthew is the horror of emperors and kings.

"Ye are the light of the world;" and there comes the further statement, that such light must not be hidden, but must be put on a lamp-stand, high, and not to be screened, so that it may give light to every one.

You cannot fail to observe that in any of the ordinary conversations or instructions of the professional ecclesiastics no such statement is made. The Saviour himself, in another place, says, "I am the light of the world,"—which is certainly true; and if you were to ask to-day, in any Sunday-school, and I think I may say in any ordinary theological school, how the world receives its light, the formal answer would be given that Jesus Christ is the light of the world. In such an answer, the remarkable expression of this text is pushed quite on one side; and if you ask those theologians who are now, even in theological circles, called the "high-and-dry people," how it happens that in this Sermon on the Mount, which they certainly regard as central and critical, — how it happens that he said to those who heard, "Ye are the light of the world," they will answer you that in that part of the address he is speaking to the company of the apostles alone. Here and now, they say, began a line of distinction between the apostles, with their successors on the one hand, and the generality of mankind on the other. They will say that the Sermon on the Mount, in speaking to our nineteenth century, says to all regularly ordained bishops, and to all people in the apostolic succession, "Ye are the light of the world;" and they give us to understand that any of us who want any light must go and light our candles at those which are held out to us by these who are selected for the business of light-bearers.

It is fair enough to answer such men according to their folly. Such men are sure to be literalists, and it is fair enough to say to them that if they mean to throw us back on the narrative, we cannot but see that the apostles were not chosen until some time after this address was delivered. Whatever authority was given to them when they were chosen, no such authority had been given to them then. And it is clear enough that the Sermon on the Mount cannot be thus subdivided into an exoteric gospel here and an esoteric gospel there. You do not turn from a statement made in a corner to a dozen men, to a statement made to the great body of disciples. No; here is an intimation, made at that central and critical moment, of what I call the democracy of the four Gospels.

The ecclesiasticism of nineteen centuries is constantly trying to brush it away. Such people as I speak of, who want to maintain that ecclesiasticism, will tell you to-day that it is not till a man formally unites himself to the church of Christ that he becomes a part of the light of the world. If you should ask at Rome, or even at Canterbury, this is what they would tell you.

Here is the reason, they would say, why it is so important to distinguish between the organized church and the outsiders. And here comes in all discussion which seems to us so queer as to a "close communion," as it is called. Those people hold to a close communion, who are afraid that without it there shall be any uncertainty as to the light which shines upon the world.

In all such matters it is quite safe to let the extravagances take care of themselves. It is as well to state them; for a frank statement, undisguised, is, in itself, their sufficient refutation. Here is the truth, as the Saviour always states it, and as it is asserting itself in the nineteenth century, in defiance of the ecclesiastics. Light is light, and because it is light it will shine; nobody can help its shining, although men can put it under a bushel. Suppose, then, that by what we call an accident, some worn-out sceptic stumbles upon a New Testament of which he knows nothing, dips into it, and reads for the first time something which is here. He gets a spark of light from it. That light will shine, and you cannot help its shining. If, when he reads, "As ye would that men should do to you, do ye so to them likewise,"—if he say, "That is good; I mean to try that;" if he do try it, why, it is a bit of light wherever he tries it. He gives light to those who are around, whoever they may be. If he go down into a gambling hell, and with the first dazed and puzzled pigeon he finds there, tries the experiment so that the poor fellow knows he tries it, why, the light shines in that hell. It shines as distinctly as it shone by the Sea of Galilee. It shines quite as distinctly as if any bishop of them all, with his mitre and his crosier, had come in there. The light is light, whoever holds the candlestick. The only danger is that which Christ himself points out, that he whose light has been lighted, does not let it shine, that he puts it into a dark lantern; or to say the same thing in Christ's own words, he hides it under a bushel.

"But," you say, "does any one hide his candle under a bushel? Pray, what is a lighted candle for?"

Why, certainly, people do. The answer is not so much of course, as you imply. We know birds are made to fly; the glory of a bird, his distinctive peculiarity, is in those glorious sweeps, and that all but utter freedom. The bird seems to defy the law of gravity itself, by which all the rest of us are chained. But some people like to take birds and shut them up in cages. That is, they like to destroy the very peculiarity which gives the birds their glory. But that is not the reason they cage them. They cage them that they may hear them sing, or that they may look on their plumage. This they could not do if the birds were soaring in mid-ether. Now, there are available reasons offered by people, who, having received the light, keep it under a bushel.

A man has a glimpse at the heavenly vision. He thinks he sees God, and he thinks he hears Him; and there *is* a temptation to stay in the forest where he heard Him, or in the garden where he saw Him, rather than to go down through the dust of the highway to do what God wants done in State street or in Chardon street. I read Thomas à Kempis yesterday morning, I read Robert Browning last night, and in each case I had a new glimpse of the celestial glory. I heard what I had never heard. I knew what I had never known. I am going to try for another such glimpse to-day. The temptation takes this form.

With Judas and Silas, and Lydia and Damaris,

last night, I read the Scriptures; we sang psalms and masses, and we really enjoyed the communion of the Spirit. We mean to enjoy it so again today; and we do not mean to risk the chance of enjoying it by troubling ourselves about sending a ton of coal for Archippus, or by taking poor Aristarchus's furniture out of pawn. Or a man says this to you: "I have no gift at helping others. I am shy and awkward. I have no success in society; but, if you will let me study, I shall forge some truth out of what is now useless ore. I can bring something to pass in my workshop, while I am useless as a tradesman, who must exchange his commodities against those of other men."

I do not like to say how far I think this delusion goes among the men of science of our time. Work in the laboratory and workshop is very tempting. Men of the very first ability will tell you they like to follow original research; they like to be testing Nature for her secrets, and gaining more light, and more. Then you ask them if they will not let this light shine before men, and they shrug their shoulders. They say, "That is another man's affair. I cannot go to address a public assembly. I have no gift in speaking to other people. I will make the light burn, but I will keep it under a bushel."

Now, some of these excuses are valid. There are plenty of good reasons why a man should, at times, withdraw to what we call absolute solitude, — to companionship with God, and God alone. To speak in our chosen figure: at the moment we strike the light, we may need to shield it on every side from the outer air. But, all the same, the light was never lighted for me alone. I must, sooner or later, put it upon a candlestick, that it may give light to all who are in the house. Yes, to all. The parable goes far, and was meant to go far, for the eternal truth goes far. From God Himself this light came, for His purpose it shines, and that purpose is infinite. And you and I are so to use our light, whatever it may be, that all men may glorify Him. This is the quaint Bible phrase — old-fashioned, if you please, and even narrow now. But it was not meant to be narrow. When I live by this central law, when I live to God's glory, what I do is done with an infinite purpose, and with an infinite result. What I say is as clear and true as if God Himself whispered it in my ear, that with my tongue I might proclaim it. No man thinks of me as the speaker, for every man knows that this is God's word which is spoken. No man thinks of me as the doer, for every man knows that this is God's work which is done. They glorify your Father which is in heaven. This is the quaint phrase. At bottom it means this, that the word and deed thus born from the Light are accepted as heavenly. They must stand; they must succeed. They mark so much progress of the world towards its heavenly condition.

It is not the high priest entering the Holy of Holies once a year who is the only light-bearer. It is the ragged boy who screens the coal as it runs down the slide into the barge. If he screen it well, if he do his duty, he also is an apostle. It is not Martin Luther or Father Hyacinthe, speaking to a thousand eager listeners who is the only light-bearer. It is the patient schoolmistress in a log cabin who is doing the best she can — "angels do no more" — with that half-naked, stupid, negro child. She also is spoken to when he says, "*Ye* are the light of the world." It is not only John Milton, or Francis de Sales, or Loyola, or Henry Martin, or Bishop Heber who has this gospel to proclaim. It is the teamster who is kind to his horses; it is the errand-boy who is on time with his letters; it is the clerk who throws up his place rather than lie across the counter: they are the light of the world. Men see their tenderness and truth, and glorify the Father who is in heaven.

I am tempted to tell you a story from the first letter which I opened this morning. It interested me the more because I was actually preparing the notes of this sermon. It was a letter from a lady in a distant city, who told me the tragedy of the life of the young fellow whom she was trying to save from the devil. She had known him as a boy, she had lost sight of him when he left home, to be an attendant — bar-tender, perhaps — in a Coney Island hotel. There, with all the temptations of such a place, the poor fellow had broken down. He had been drunk, he had gambled away all his earnings, — let us hope he had not gambled away those of anybody else. And so, broken down, in rags and disgrace, he comes back to his old friend. She tells me the story of this and that act of tenderness by which she has tried to reclaim him; and — he and she together, for the last nine or ten months — he has trampled the scorpions and serpents under his feet, and so far stands erect. Is he to stand erect? Is he to overcome the enemy who has been too much for him before? I wrote her this morning that, if he is to succeed, it must be by trying to help somebody else. He must let his light shine before men. He must not keep it under a bushel. If he himself can rescue some other poor dog from the temptations around him, as she has rescued him, then there is a hope for him, for he also is in the apostleship. And he ought to know that he is in the apostleship. It is his place as much as it is hers. It is hers just as much as it is that of any priest; just as the priest ought to know that it is his as much as if he were bishop; and the bishop ought to know that it is his as much as if he were a pope. It is the place of every one to let his light shine.

These are only illustrations, and those not on a large scale, of the steady increase of the volume and sway of light, if light will only shine. And when we rise from the image to speak of The Light, — the light that shines for every heart and for all mankind, — we leave wholly behind us these little illustrations. You who have seen God, you who have heard Him, you who have loved man, yes, and have helped him, — you are the light of the world. Not only the saint who sees God always! It is you as well, though you never had but one flash of the vision. Do your duty, as God works with you, and then your light will so shine that all men will see that here is God; that God is, and rules. And this is what is bidden. More than teaching children their letters: it is the showing children how to live. More, indeed, than reading and writing: it is living, loving, growing in life; succeeding. It is living with a purpose. It is loving all mankind. The true hero, the true prophet, as you always find at last, may not be a man accomplished in methods or forms. He may not know his letters, and may not be able to teach them. But so he lives to God's glory, so he carries out God's purpose; his light shines. Because it shines, it makes other lives brighter and easier. They live, their light shines, yet others live and other light shines. And more and more do men know that the power which makes for righteousness sways the world more and more completely. For you

His kingdom comes, and for me, whether we have come to hear our Saviour from dusty and formal Jerusalem, or from the sea-breezes of Tyre and Sidon, the one thing, simplest and easiest, is to live with men and for men, so as to carry farther God's work and purpose. Freely ye have received, freely give. This is the Saviour's statement, in another place, of this same duty. I have been taught the golden rule. I know the beatitudes to be the truth. I have read the word which cannot die. I have seen the Life of lives. I will not be so mean as to let eighteen centuries give me this, and, for myself, to give nothing to the men and women round me, who do not know, who have not felt, who have not seen, and do not understand. I will not read the daily record of misery in the paper without any effort to help somewhere. I will not see that black sheet of crime without an effort to save somebody. Somewhere, somehow, I can make this eternal light so shine, that somebody shall know God better than he knows Him now, and shall live in more perfect joy and allegiance to His perfect will.

This is the Saviour's system of an apostleship. Whether it began with twelve, or seventy, or five thousand, is nothing. It appeals now to every life, so soon as any life hears, sees, or knows. Do you know anything of love? make others love. Do you know anything of truth? make others true.

Is life worth living to you? make others' lives worth living to them. For it is as true to you in Boston as to those in Syria, that you are the salt of the world. How wretched if that salt lose its savor — worthless! You are the light of the world. So let your light shine before men, that as they see your good works, they may glorify your Father which is in heaven.

PHILLIPS BROOKS.

(*A sermon delivered on the Sunday after his death.*)

IN all that I say in the great loss which we have sustained, I know that I am speaking as a personal friend. And you who listen have the same feeling of personal regard for Phillips Brooks. It is a pleasure to you that you have lived in the same town with him; that you have met him in the street; that you know the cadences of his voice. There is not a person here who knew anything about him, who would not have gone to him in any difficulty: sure, first of all, of his sympathy; confident, next, of wise advice; and probably he would have given of his own time and effort to carry you through your difficulty.

In this tender personal relation between us and him, we are wholly unable to look upon his life as if he were on the other side of the world. We cannot analyze the methods of his daily duty; we cannot compare him with other men who had like things to do. And we are very glad we cannot. We are sorrowing for a friend, thinking of a friend, and describing a friend. We cannot place him in any perspective of history, and we do not want to. We cannot say how or why he affected us, and we do not want to. We have lost a dear friend, and we stop each other on the street to say so.

For myself, I have not the slightest recollection of the time when I first knew him. It seems as if I had always known him. I suppose I first met him when he was a school-boy in the Latin School, somewhat shy, he says himself, but still a favorite with his friends, and taking, like other boys, the joys and trials of boy life. In the Civil War, which cuts across the lives of all of us who had come to manhood, — as a trap-dyke cuts through layers of all ages, — in the Civil War he was holding Philadelphia up to its duty; and young as he was, was teaching the most aristocratic of churches how democratic is the gospel of Jesus Christ. He must have blessed God, as all of us do, for the great opportunity and the great training of the four years of the war. To wake every morning with a definite duty for the whole; perhaps to stand by the corpse of your brother, who has died that others may live; to feel yourself in a hundred crises that you would die so gladly if so you could save the nation. This is to have religion taught in an object-lesson such as you young men and women do not find so easily. He was all linked in with sanitary work, hospital work, recruiting work, work of education, freedman's aid, refugees' aid, and, young as he was, everybody knew he was a power.

"Perhaps then first he understood Himself, how wondrously endued."

Certainly he must have learned then what are the immense advantages of the position of a clergyman, in a crisis where it is his duty to have a share in every endeavor, no matter how different from that of the hour before. To provide, in the morning, bed, blankets, and coffee for regiments hurried from the North to the front; at noon to provide stretchers and ambulances to the wounded carried to their homes — literally, to stanch their blood; in the evening to receive and find homes for starving black women sent North by some puzzled army commissary; to choose teachers and send school-books for the children of those women left half orphans on their islands; to pack ether, surgical instruments, and perhaps playing-cards, to be used by prisoners in the Libby; to send vaccine virus to an army corps in Louisiana; and all the time to be stating in public on Sunday, and on every other day, the eternal truths which were at issue; to hold up a wayward and anxious public; to comfort those that mourn; to encourage the despondent; to keep clear the vision of the possible future; — such infinite variety of duty seems wellnigh impossible to a man in any other calling. It may well puzzle or dismay any man who is trained only to a specialty, like a machinist, an inventor, a mere man of letters, or merchant, or mechanic, or chemist, or investor. But the glory of our calling is that it is not a specialty. It is wrong to say, as at our ordinations they are apt to say, that we are "set apart." We are enjoined not to go apart, by infinite injunction; not to go apart or to be apart. We are servants, ministers. And that not simply to this church, or to that hospital, or to yonder prison, but literally to all sorts and conditions of men. Of such universal service Phillips Brooks had doubtless dreamed when he was a student. But the war, with its thousands of activities, showed him that no dream of such universal service could be too grand.

I see, and hear, and read all the time explanations of his greatness. People please themselves with analyses of his power. We do not make much of such efforts. They relieve, perhaps, a little the sense of loss. They give a certain outside machinery for sympathy. But the simple truth remains, that here is a great man. He is a great man because he is a simple, humble, unselfish son of God, alive with God's life and engaged in God's affair. This is clear, that he is intimate in the closest way with the going and coming of the well-beloved Son of God, whom he has chosen as his nearest friend and his best counsellor. For the rest, he cares little for himself, thinks little of himself, and, as I believe, knows very little of himself. He is always surprised when people speak of him with enthusiasm. He does not know why they want to hear him speak, and imagines that other people can say the same thing just as well as he does. Such is always the characteristic of a great man. He does these things which surprise and delight the rest of us as if they are entirely of course, — as to him indeed they are. And so he wonders that every one else does not do the same.

When we say, then, that here is a great man, this is really not because he is a great preacher, or because he writes so well, or because he knows what he thinks, or because he says what he knows. It is just the other way. He is a great preacher because he is a great man. He says what he thinks because he is a great man. He binds as with a spell the group of young men he talks to because he is a great man. And, because he is a great man, he would have done anything else it was his business to do in the fashion of a master. If he had had to organize emigration, he would have organized it well. If he had had to open a railway to the Pacific, he would have done it well. He is one of those who understands that it is easier and better to do a great thing than a little one.

Now, this means that this man is at work on the infinite lines. He is not satisfied with any "say-so" of the cyclopædia, or any poor rule-of-thumb. You never heard him repeat a commonplace in a speech. Always he gave you a fundamental principle, the special bit of eternity, on which that transaction rested. It has always seemed to me, when I met him on any public occasion, that he was absolutely careless as to what the schools call a " preparation for an address." He prepared, but not as they prepare. He did not seem to care for the beginning, the middle, or the end, whether it had any beginning, middle, or end. What he cared for was the special direction of the dear God who had sent him about that particular bit of business. He wanted us to see that as plainly as he saw it; and almost always we did see it. We went home thanking God that we did see it. We knew for that once at least that God had spoken to us, and had inspired this special son of His to be His spokesman. When you have thus been led in the line of infinite Life by such a leader, you do not care much for any definition or analysis which explains to you in what senses he is to be called a great man.

This should be said, however, and I say it as definitely as I can, because it has not been said as I wanted to hear it: This man, with all his power, understood as well as any man that he must do what he had to do in the right way. Thus, he did not speak without knowing perfectly what he was going to say. He never relied on any gush, or enthusiasm, or personal magnetism, or spontaneous utterance, or the stimulus of a crowded audience. He never insulted an audience, even the smallest and humblest, without — in his way — preparing himself carefully to address them. It is a great pity that all public speakers cannot say the same thing.

His way was to determine carefully, in advance, what was the most important principle involved; so you were perfectly certain when you went to hear him, that you were going to hear something worthy of your careful thought and memory.

He was, therefore, from early life, a diligent student. Some one said he was an omnivorous reader when he was a boy; and it is interesting to see — what you will see in all his books — how much he managed to read in the midst of his active duty, in this most active of callings. Nor was this helter-skelter and miscellaneous reading; — it was reading on distinct lines which he knew to be his own. Thus, in his valuable Essay on Biography, he treats the whole subject as Mr. Lowell might treat it, or any man of letters, with the ease of one who has himself done what he is recommending to others.

It is the fashion to say that though he was a profoundly religious man, he was no theologian. This seems to me quite untrue. No man has his power who does not know very well what he thinks, what he feels, and what he knows about the eternities. It seems to me, on the other hand, that he had studied with conscientious care the great questions, — of which there are not many, — and had early arrived at some conclusions so

definite that they were not easily distributed. He
was in the theological school early enough to feel
the last waves of what we call the "Oxford Controversy." He knew what both sides said, and
rated what they said at its worth. But such a
man knew, of course, all the time, that there are
realities far more important than the embroidering of an altar-cloth or the links in an historical
line of succession. Those realities are what interested him. Of all the writers of our time who
had helped him and led him, I think he would
have named James Martineau as the first. You
find traces of Martineau in all that he says, as you
do in the thoughtful work of all the great religious
teachers who now use the English language. His
theology, then, is the theology of all the active
church in all the communions of Christianity in
this end of the nineteenth century. It is the
same for all the theology of the Holy Spirit,
or of the Real Presence. These are the Scripture
phrases. In the modern phrase, it is the theology
of the immanent presence of God. It is the
theology of "Immanuel," — "God with *us*,"
not the mediæval theology of God with one man.
In his absolute faith in the Real Presence, he felt
and understood what was the presence of God
with Jesus of Nazareth. He saw how that presence, felt and acknowledged, made Jesus of
Nazareth the Saviour of mankind. He saw that
Jesus of Nazareth would have lived and died

unknown, like millions of others of God's sons, but that he felt, knew, and said that the word he spoke was God's word, his act was God's act, and his gospel God's command. That nothing in his life was of any value, but as it proclaimed to men this immanent presence of God. God here and God now. "The kingdom of God is at hand." But Mr. Brooks knew and felt all this of Jesus because, and as he knew and felt, that God is now always with each and all of His children. The Incarnation for him is no three-years wonder of Nazareth and Jerusalem. It is the central necessity of all human life in all time. To-day, as in the day of Tiberius, in Boston as in Sychar, or in Capernaum, "if ye seek me, surely ye shall find me, if ye seek for me with all your hearts."

With this certainty as to the Real Presence, he places at their real value many details about which little men quarrel. But he knows that the quarrel is interesting to them, and so he will not speak of them contemptuously. And this remark covers that broad tolerance of his which annoys and perplexes so many who love him most. He passes by some little things, as I pass by the mistakes in accent of a Frenchman or a German with whom I talk, though they be mistakes which a teacher of language would be bound to correct every time he heard them. With his enthusiasm for Maurice, Kingsley, Stanley, Fremantle, Tait, and such men who have led the

Established Church of England out into the path of freedom, he is willing to accept as interesting antiquities certain mediæval phrases, and even mediæval customs, not for what they are now, but for what they have been. The tattered pine-tree flag, which fluttered over the redoubt at Bunker Hill, is not now the symbol of any State or nation. But it was that day. And because it was that day, I bear the rag reverently in my procession, and I preserve it for another festival in my most sacred casket. So is it that these scholars preserve this or that old bit of costume, whether in a creed, in a robe, or a stained-glass window. It is all one. And you must not take them to task, even if they use in old ritual service words of David, which a boy in the streets of any Christian city to-day would be ashamed to use.[1] You must not take them to task, more than you take me to task for the impossible anatomy of the wings of the angel in the window yonder. Such men, when they are large enough to know the reality of religion, think they can afford to disregard what they call infelicities of old-fashioned expression. It is the little men who are injured by playing with rusty tools:—the men who do not know what religion is, the men who study machinery with no knowledge of power; the men who have studied crutches and cork legs until they do not know what an athlete is doing when he runs a race. It is such

---

[1] See Psalm cxxxvii. 9, for instance.

men for whom outgrown creeds and archaic rituals work certain disaster and irretrievable ruin.

All this is to say again, at more length than is needed, that he has brought the largest motive to the management of daily duty. A child of God, he found out what it is to love God as Father, and early in life went loyally about his Father's business. To this he consecrates life very early in his career. To do it he makes himself all at home in the life of that first-born Son of God, who first used those words, "I must be about my Father's business," and who lived and died that men may know who God is; that He is here; that they can work or play, think and enjoy, as His children do, as those who are born from Him and share His nature. He starts on his career with such consecration, and it proves that he has the power which you would suppose. Cheerful? Yes, because he enters into the joy of Him in whose life he lives: "My joy shall remain with you, and your joy be full." Even of temper? Yes, level-headed and easy in harness; for he has infinite power, and people who have that, are not apt to fret about failure. Ready to wait, to bide his time? Why not? Have we not eternity before us? Modest, unassuming? Of course he does not do these things as if he had taught himself or had learned how. It is your Father who tells us what to do and how to speak. Fond of the young? I should suppose he would be, seeing we are all so many children in our Father's house, going on our Father's errands. Indifferent as to social rank, high or low, rich or poor? How can he keep it, he who is of the Blood Royal, and used every day to the dignity of the palace? Indifferent as to death? That follows when one has undertaken an immortal's career.

Born in a city whose elegant people train themselves on system to find fault and complain, he never found fault with anything or anybody. If you only met him in the street or talked with him at a party, you saw that he found life well worth living. And I suppose this is the great lesson he has taught to younger men. It might be a tread-mill to others, but he knew where his patient steps led and what was the path on which he trod. When his boys were with him they knew that life was worth living. Stupid, formal, in the rut, if you only thought of yourself, your income, your clothes, your food, your investment, your horse, or your hound. But not formal, not stupid, not monotonous, if you knew where it led you and why you were alive. Some of you will remember that parable which he used one night at the Union. He led them into the doorway at the bottom of the great monument yonder. What is there before them? Only a few steps in sight to be mounted. Indeed, there is nothing for it but to step on them; no right hand, and no left. Round and round in one damned monotony, you say. Round and round, — so tedious, so tiresome, the tenth like the first, the twentieth like the tenth. Still round and round, because it is to-day's duty; round and round, because my Father bids me. I hold on. I do not criticise; I do not complain. Round and round; it will not last as long as I shall. Round and round, and of a sudden it proves I have been mounting on a spiral all the time, higher and higher in my round and round. The sacred, solemn moment comes. They call it death. I believe it is life, when I see that my faithful duty, day by day, has lifted me where, in the broad sunlight of heaven, I look out on the eternities. I am in the centre of the infinite horizon. I hear the infinite harmonies. Yes, I see God.

When his great master and dear friend Stanley died, Dr. Brooks said what we may well say of him:

"These lessons will be taught by many lives in many languages before the end will come; but for many years yet to come there will be men who will find not the least persuasive and impressive teaching of them in Dean Stanley's life. The heavens will still be bright with stars, and younger men will never miss the radiance which they never saw. But for those who once watched for his light there will always be a spot of special darkness in the heavens where a star of special beauty went out when he died."

CREED AND LIFE.

"Why call ye me, Lord, Lord, and do not the things which I say?" LUKE vi. 46.

CHRISTIANITY is a life, and not a creed.

This epigram has been a favorite statement of the more liberal writers and speakers of the church for the last half-century. And as these men animate and control the whole church in all its communions, more and more this statement, or something like it, is heard everywhere.

It seems that I used it, I know not where, in some public address six or eight months ago. So I found it challenged, very courteously, in one of the least extravagant Catholic journals, when I returned to Boston. The editor, or one of his friends, kindly sent me the criticism. Substantially, it was this: "Whatever a man says about it, he must have a creed. Dr. Hale wants men to live well. Somebody, then, must define what living well is. That definition is a creed. You may say Christianity is a life, if you like; but so long as you call that life Christianity, you imply that there is a Christian creed behind it."

This criticism, good-natured and courteous in its tone, seems to me to belong to that playing with words which is the special danger with men educated in colleges, or in any other sort of cloisters, without knowing much of affairs. The importance thus attached to words, symbols, or what in politics we call platforms, has brought disaster a hundred times to the Roman Catholic Church, not to say to all other closely organized churches. But as this statement is repeated by a certain school of men, with the best intention, and with the idea that it is important, I suppose that it ought to be considered in any series of sermons on the conduct of life.

I do not know who first uttered in the English language the particular expression challenged: " Christianity is a life, and not a creed." I thought at one time that the phrase was James Martineau's, and I think I have said so here; but some one — and I am not sure but that it was Dr. Martineau himself — has told me he thought that the phrase could be found in Channing's writings. I do not know, and I do not care, except that I want to correct any statement which I have made under a false impression.

What it means, when we of the liberal churches make it, is not the statement that there is no such reality as Law. On the other hand, we are very anxious to say that there is a right way of life and a wrong way of life. The right way of life is indicated by Christianity, which is absolute religion. The wrong way of life is well-nigh certain when a man has no religion at all. And when we say that Christianity is a life, and not a creed, we mean exactly what Jesus Christ meant when he said, "I am the Way, the Truth, and the Life." He did not say, "I am the law, the statement, and the creed." On the other hand, he said a great many hard things about people who relied upon written statements, inherited laws, and formal creeds. And here it is an interesting thing to observe, that for nearly a generation of men, what we call Christianity, or the Christian religion, was not called by those names; but it was called "The Way" or "The Road," so distinct was the understanding on all sides that it was a way or road in which people were to travel, and that union in it was to be shown by what people did in their lives, and not what they said with their tongues.[1]

In nineteen centuries of history, nineteen-twentieths of the ecclesiastics of the world, being men educated in the midst of books and fond of them, have felt and have said that the necessity of Christianity is a good verbal statement of its purpose and system. Apostles' Creed, Nicene Creed, Athanasian Creed, Canons of the Fifteen Councils, Decrees of the Council of Trent, Thirty-nine Articles, Westminster Confession, and, literally, a thousand more such symbols, are monuments of the interest which the ecclesiastics of

---

[1] "Way" does not mean "manner" or "method," as it means with us; but, literally, a path or a roadway.

the world have taken in creeds or statements. But all this time these formal statements have not advanced one man or one woman one inch in The Way or in the Christian life. The Christian life has been advanced when some widow took an orphan baby into her hovel on the side of the Viminal; when St. Vincent took the place of a criminal on the bench of a galley; when Philip Sydney, dying, gave a cup of water to the soldier in more pain than he; when this or that unnamed physician has gone into this or that hospital of contagion, and died in the performance of his duty. And what we mean when we say that Christianity is a life, and not a creed, is, that Christianity must be avouched, illustrated, and extended by action; — that Christianity is as dead and as silent when it is only expressed in creeds, as a stereotyped plate, even of the Bible, is when it is buried in a vault under a sidewalk, or as the record of a phonograph is if nobody sets the roller in motion. And we have very high authority in Christian history for saying this. We have the authority of the Apostle Paul, when he says "the letter killeth, but the Spirit giveth life." That is a very strong statement. It is as if I should say, "Every time you repeat the Nicene Creed without Spirit, without the Holy Spirit, it kills you. You are, to all intents and purposes, a decaying corpse, when you say such things by rote without the inspiration of the present Holy

Spirit of the loving God." And we have the authority of the Saviour himself, when he said in this text, "Why call ye me, Lord, Lord, and do not the things which I say?" That is a very short creed which is shut up in the four letters L-O-R-D; but he hated that, though it implied personal regard for him, personal confidence, — if you please, personal enthusiasm, — so long as they did not in visible action carry out the purpose of God for which he was living. It is very suggestive and it is very important that he never says, "Assent to this statement." He even says, "You may believe my words or not, as you like, so you only believe that the things I do are genuine." What he does exact of each and all of them is not in the words "Obey me," not in the words "Listen to me," but in the words "Follow me." That is, they are to show in a visible and positive act that they are walking in his way. And that is substantially what we mean whenever we say that Christianity is a life, and not a creed.

So firmly seated, however, in the minds of educated people is this determination that everything shall be said before it is done that Cardinal Newman actually refused to treat the question of what primitive Christianity was until it had been scientifically stated. "The hypothesis [of an early corruption of Christianity] has no claims on our attention till it is drawn out scientifically, till we are informed what the Christian doctrine is."[1] One is reminded of the old joke on people of sixteen quarterings who are supposed to say, "Let us be genteel or die." "Let us be scientific or die," seems to us freelances as absurd.

But the leaders of liberal Christianity have never been unwilling to accept the challenge. They say, and their followers say,— among whom I say,— that a sufficient definition of a Christian is following Christ, and that if any man makes the effort to follow Christ, whether he expresses this in any formula of words or not, he is a Christian. I say still more, that it is of no consequence whether he be called a Christian or not, so he be living in that divine Spirit in which Jesus Christ lived. Why, he may be an inhabitant of a continent beyond the Antarctic ice, where the name of Jesus Christ was never heard, and where he has been brought to this absolute knowledge of God by other means.

When we are pressed, or asked if we cannot give in words a definition of what it is to follow Christ, we say we can We interest ourselves, however, in seeing in how few words this can be said; and I may say, in passing, that it would seem as if the mechanical churches had devoted their attention to seeing how many words the same definition may require. I said to the late Freeman Clarke once that I had succeeded in bringing the verbal defini-

---

[1] Introduction to Development of Christian Doctrine, p. 18. American edition.

tion of Christianity into six words. He answered that he was in advance of me, for he had long since brought it down to four. His four words were, "Love God, love man." My six words were, "With God, for man, in heaven." I wanted, as you all here know, to say that faith, love, and hope are the whole; perhaps I might have been satisfied with Paul's statement, where he says, "These three abide and continue forever."

Now, when we say that Christianity is a life, and not a creed, we mean that whether a person can read a creed or not, whether he have been taught it in words or not, if he sees the Christian life he can enter into it and follow it. We mean, as I said, just what the Saviour meant when he insisted upon action instead of expression. And it is very interesting to see, in his own personal history, how closely he held himself to his own statement. Take that most pathetic conversation with the young nobleman of Edom. So far as verbal expression went, he and the Saviour were at one; the young man says, almost sadly, "I have kept the Ten Commandments; that is, I have obeyed the written law, from my youth up." Jesus tells him what is the one thing that he needs. The one thing he needs, it seems, is action. "Follow me; do as I do; lift up that which has fallen down; bring comfort where there is no comfort; make men see and know that the kingdom of God is at hand." All the established churches, when young men come to them who wish to be ministers of this gospel, say, " Yes, if you will go into such and such a school and study such and such languages and read such and such books, and pass an examination in those books, at the end of such and such a time we will give you a license which shall enable you to go out and say to all the world that the kingdom of God is at hand." But Jesus Christ took no such precautions for good grammar or for conservative utterance. He found some fishermen washing their nets; he did not say to them, " Learn anything," but he said, " Follow me." He found a man changing money at the tax-broker's stall, and he did not say to him, " Learn anything," but, " Follow me." There is not the slightest indication that one of the twelve apostles had made any study whatever in the formulas of the Jewish church, or of the Christian church that was to be. They were simply men who, as he thought, had pluck and energy enough for the position to which he was to appoint them, who had followed him so far that he knew something about them, and whom he therefore appointed, because they were men of action, for the emergency.

I cited on Wednesday night the remarkable illustration of the same principle, in the lives of three unnamed Roman soldiers. There is one man of whom the Saviour says, "I have not found such faith, no, not in Israel." He had not found it among these Pharisees and scribes, learned in the law; he had not found it in the high court of appeal, the Seventy, where he knew Nicodemus personally; he had not found it in the little court of Herod, tetrarch of Galilee; he finds it in a centurion in the Roman army. So, at the cross, when all his friends have deserted him, when the mob of Jerusalem has turned against him, with his mother and her friends weeping at his side, the unnamed centurion in command, whose soldiers have wrought the sacrifice, says, " Truly this is a righteous man; truly this is the Son of God." Once more, after he has himself left the world, when the church is left to the direction of the present Spirit, when the question comes whether this Way of Life is to be one more sect of Judaism or to be the absolute religion of the world, it is left to a Roman soldier to solve that question with Saint Peter. He sends to Peter to come and tell him what is the Way of Life; and Peter comes, and the notion of a peculiar people, or a church separate from mankind, is broken down forever. In these three critical instances, it is men of action, and not men of words, who present to us the ideal of the Christian life.

To me it is at once pathetic and interesting to see how, in the face of its scholars and creed-makers, the church, in practice, is, almost unwillingly, forced into the same line, if it means to preserve its existence. As Dr. Wayland said once, "Christianity has no defensive armor; it must be on the aggressive, or it is lost." This is absolutely true. What are called the evidences of Christianity become the defences of Christianity, and then, in the phrase of the last century, the apologies for Christianity. On the other hand, ask any person, partial or impartial, where it is that he is interested in the history of this religion, and you find he has got hold of Xavier, going out from Europe to press the new life in Ceylon and Japan; you find he has some story of the Moravians planting their missions of love on the coast of Labrador or in the West Indies. Dr. Storrs, of the American Board of Commissioners of Foreign Missions, said to me once, and I think said with truth, that if the Congregational Church of New England had established its great missionary system earlier, he believed the Great Schism would have been prevented. By the Great Schism he meant the separation of that Congregational body into the two houses, Orthodox and Heterodox, — a separation which does not do any great harm, perhaps, but which certainly does not do a great deal of good. He meant, what he did not say, that if the church had shown herself in action in the period between 1810 and 1825, most men would have forgotten the rigmarole of the Five Points of Calvin, — rigmarole which leads to idolatry or to infidelity. And so of any Christian saint, — those who fill the calendar of the

Roman Church, or those, perhaps, who belonged to no established church, people like John Milton or Roger Williams, whose names have not been written on the calendar of any ecclesiastical organization, — if they have done the things that the Lord said, if they have lived in his spirit, if they have followed in his Way, they have wrought the miracle. There is another of Dr. Wayland's epigrams: some one asked him, of one of his distinguished friends, if he thought that he was a Christian. His answer was, "Can he drive out the devils? If he can, he meets all my requisitions or the Master's." He referred, of course, to the passage in the Gospels where the disciples told Jesus that they had rebuked one whom they found casting out devils in his name. They rebuked him, as ecclesiastics rebuke such people to-day, "because he walketh not with us." And Jesus said, "Forbid him not. No man can work a miracle in my name, and lightly speak evil of me."

And the Master is willing that his church shall stand the test to which he leaves fisherman, apostle, young nobleman, and repentant sinner. It is the test of kings, and emperors, and fishermen, of preachers and blacksmiths, of artists and dressmakers, — the simple test of thistles, and vines and fig-trees. All of them — the emperor and the blacksmith — shall be judged by their fruits. The fishing-net and the church will be judged by what they do. The doctrine will be judged by the life. The life will not be judged by the doctrine. At this plan of his the doctrine-makers will be dissatisfied. The men of words will skilfully twist words, to say it were better the other way. You and I — how gladly would we get over the need of travelling ten miles on foot this morning, if it would answer to say we have done it. But it will not answer. To live as one lives who knows that God is here has not proved to be easy. To say, "I believe in God, the Father Almighty," has proved to be very easy. Millions of people say it every Sunday morning. The Saviour of mankind was not pleased when they said it, unless they did it; unless they showed their belief in their act. "Why call ye me, Lord, Lord, and do not the things which I say?" His religion is not a creed, it is a life.

THE LAW OF LOVE.

"On these two commandments hangeth the whole law, and the prophets." MATT. xxii. 40.

THE two are co-related, — as modern science is fond of saying.

I have spoken here twice, this winter, on the New Englander's determined habit to achieve something every day. It is what his Catechism calls "living to the glory of God."

This hard determination, so utterly unlike the indifference of the savage whom he displaced, has been thought to produce an angular and unyielding habit of life. The New Englander has the name of being as certain and unchanging as the north-west winds, and of being as cold and generally disagreeable. And there is many a critic who would say, "Give us less determination, if you only will give us more tenderness."

We who are here should never admit that such a complaint can fairly be made of the New Englander of to-day. But none the less is it our business to ask, in any such study of righteous life as we are making here this winter, how this north-west wind of energy and truth and right is tempered in the Christian scheme. It will not do to have the name "Puritan" regarded as the synonym of *stern* or *pitiless*. We must not let what the Scotch call the "unco guid" people, make goodness disagreeable. And, for our own lives, we must not let determination, consecration, and duty claim all the majesty and certainty of law, while tenderness, gentleness, and the forgiveness of injuries are supposed to be left to the accident of whim, or convenience, or other happenings. That is a critical and central text which, in describing our good God, says, "Mercy and truth have met together; righteousness and peace have kissed one another." If such absolute union of firmness and tenderness are to be found in the Father, why, they must be found, as a rule, in you and me, who are His children.

And I ought to say, at the very outset, that so far as the New Testament goes, — as original and simple Christianity goes, — there never has been any doubt about this union. From the early centuries comes that happy proverb of the outsiders, "Behold how these Christians love one another!"[1] Puritans may be called hard and austere; Methodists may be laughed at as narrow; New Church people and Baptists may be called clannish; Episcopalians may be laughed at for the absurdity of their harmless formalities; but Christians, pure and simple, were in the beginning, as they ought to be now, cheerful, affectionate, good-tempered, good-humored, good-natured. Partners of

---

[1] Tertullian's Apologeticus.

Omnipotence, they take life easily. Sure that they are in God's law, they know it will work without jar or friction. They need not be fussing about more oil on this pivot, or less strain on that bearing. Least of all, will any one of them be downcast or distressed because he supposes he has the universe to care for.

All this is shown in the Epistles. In John's letters, the absolute necessity of our mutual love takes the place of all other injunctions about duty. Mercy is justice. In the practical summing up in James's letter, he demands personal purity first. The tool must be as good as God made it. Then, in an overflowing stream of words, all meaning Love, he names peace, gentleness — "the Christian is easy to be entreated; he is full of mercy and good fruits." You might say, that is the whole of it.

And it is here, and in one or two parallel passages in Paul's letters, that there comes in that admirable description of a gentleman. It ought to be written in letters of gold in the schools and colleges. A gentleman is one who gladly remits something from his rights.[1] He does not stick for the letter of the bond. He does not exact the last blot of blood.

[1] I cannot find this admirable phrase earlier than in J. F. Schleusner's Lexicon, Leipsic, 1808. This is in the reference to Paul's statement as to bishops: "libenter cedentem, et de jure duo libenter remittentem." But it must have been put into epigrammatic language long before Schleusner's time.

I do not remember who first called Saint Paul "the prince of gentlemen;" but the remark is perfectly true, and we cannot bear it in mind too often as we read his letters. And then, coming back from the Epistles to the Gospels, nothing is more clear than that the attitude of Jesus to all those who were around him was that of one who was making religion cheerful, and rescuing it from the gloom, as he rescued it from the pettiness, of the formalists. That he "went about eating and drinking" was the sneer of the Pharisees; that the "common people heard him gladly" was the report of the policemen. Renan calls his life in Galilee "a summer idyl;" and nothing is more certain than that the welcome which he met was that of those who recognized that his news was indeed "glad tidings." Indeed, the proclamation of absolute religion always effects a complete revolution or upheaval from all mechanical and material types of religion. Of this revolution there is no visible token more distinct than that which makes religion the central power of the joy and strength of life; or, as we say here so often, compels man, the child, to enter into the life of his Father.

Now, our affair this morning is to bring into our management of daily life those master considerations which, as eternal principles, so govern every detail of life that we shall never drop back into that mistake of the sour Puritan of the second generation. I say "the Puritan of the second generation," for when we remember that such light-hearted persons as Philip Sidney, and even William Shakespeare,[1] would probably have been marked as Puritans by the men of their time; when we remember that John Milton, who was no ascetic, and who knew how to enjoy life, was Puritan of the Puritans, — we understand more distinctly that the familiar censure now passed on Puritanism did not always belong to it. This is very perfectly shown in Macaulay's paper, as the contempt, unjustly piled in later days, upon the Roundheads and others, to whom we owe all the blessings of constitutional liberty. Rightly considered, law is not a bit of external compulsion; but when it does its perfect work, it is the interior principle of life. When, in the Lord's Prayer, we ask that God's will may be done on earth as it is done in heaven, we are asking that His life may absorb and control our lives, and that all movement of human affairs may be as gentle, as regular, and as agreeable as are the movements of the planets in the universe. Language is full of epigrams which express this. The poets, as well as the astronomers, see that the planets and meteors move in curves and not in straight lines. There are no sudden breaks and angles; this was early observed, and the poets constantly remind us of it.

---

[1] There is an interesting paper by Leonard Withington on this point in his volumes of essays called "The Puritan."

Of which observation, the value, or the interior meaning, is, that there is no shock nor conflict, no sudden surprise or instant variation of will, but that the motion of nature is a movement smooth and even. Now, such external expressions of the poets are of use, if they show us what is the condition of our lives when regulated by and from an interior principle, which subdues the processes of life, and which, on the other hand, makes them strong and effective: if thus we can break down that tradition of the puppet-show, which supposes that the Director of life pulls us hither and thither by strings and wires. Of such pulling and hauling, the jerky results are not like the movement of the heavens of God, but are like the contrivance of some inferior being, who has not reason to feel the sense of law.

The physicists of to-day are fond of saying that all the laws of Nature may be reduced to two: the law of attraction and the law of heat. Without asking the tempting question whether these two may be reduced to one, let us try to familiarize ourselves with this statement in the details of the exhibition of law. Gravitation does not work by starts or fits; there is not gravitation in this minute, and no gravitation in the next minute, with more gravitation in the third minute. It is a constant, steady force, always and absolutely to be relied upon, and working with such precision that the orbit is always the same orbit, the sweep of the smoke across the sky is always in harmonious curves, and the ascent of the balloon, if you know the conditions, may be predetermined. So of the law of heat. Heat produces so much expansion from such an amount of heat, or, from such an amount of heat I can develop such an amount of electricity; and this, as before, by no hitches or starts, by no sudden impulse, but with that absolute steadiness which indeed belongs to the very name of law, if we would only use words carefully and distinctly.

Now, the new impulse which the Christian religion gave to the world was in making the absolute statement that the life and work of man also may be governed thus by law, by a law, by one law, by the infinite law, by the same law which governs planets, governs worlds, and governs universes. Simply, the details of human life may be governed by the law of God; or, as the Saviour says all along, man is the child of God, and may partake the nature of God, if only he will. Now, as orbits belong to the law of gravitation, what is the law to which the life of separate human beings belongs? The first statement to be made about it is that men's life is a common life. They depend upon each other as much as the cells in the leaves of a tree depend upon each other. Precisely as you cannot have one living leaf-cell unless it be linked in with a million, precisely so you cannot have one living man unless he be linked in with millions of living men. His life their life, their life is his life. And if he means to govern his life at all, to govern it rightly and well, he must govern it with a consciousness of this constant central principle of life which binds him to all living men and women, and makes them indeed, as we say so fondly, one family in their Father's love.

It is true that, if you find a savage or a child who is ignorant of this law of the common life, it is perhaps easier to teach him that this thing is right, that that thing is right, that this statement is true, that that statement contradicts eternal truth; — it may be easier at the beginning that he shall get this sense of righteousness or justice, of which men speak so fondly, and to which in general they ascribe the characteristics of law. And my hard Puritan comes as far as this. He talks of righteousness, he talks of justice, and he talks of truth; but I must own that he is a little apt to talk of them as if they asserted their power from the outside, as he incorrectly supposes that the lightning asserts its power in the changes of a thunder-storm. The truth is that there was just as much electricity in the world and in life, when he was sailing on the smooth surface of a summer sea, as there is when he sees these flashes of lightning in the midst of darkness and tempest. And so is it true that there is as much law, — the law of love and gentleness in the midst of hard righteousness, stern truth, and invincible justice, as there is when he sees a mother kiss her child, or any other of the displays of what he is pleased to call mercy. What he needs is to understand that truth, righteousness, and justice do belong to the eternal sympathy which should bind all men and women together, and which will bind them together when the daily prayer is answered, and God's will is done by men and women who are His children as it is done by Him in the majesty of that infinite life which it pleases us to call Heaven.

The Puritan gentleman, or the gentle Puritan, — you may call him what you will, — lives for the common welfare. In organizing his State he gives it the name of the "Commonwealth." It is true that whether other men ask of a man who is his father, what does he know, how much is he worth, the Puritan asks, "What has he done?" and he means "what has he done for the common interest." That picture which we had at the Club, of the public work of Johnson and Winthrop and Dudley in the beginning, was well spoken of as the omen and prophecy of the work of the Puritan gentleman for the city of his home. And he invents the phrase "Public Spirit," — the public breath, the life-breath of the community, — as a phrase to express the life-breath of every man and woman in the State. When a man dies who has challenged attention, the question such men ask is as to his public spirit. Mr. Weld,

General Butler, Mr. Morse, the reporter who died on duty, they all have to pass the same inquiry, Did he live for others, or did he live and die for himself? Was he a man of public spirit? or, did she know she was one in the Commonwealth? All this means that at bottom, in human affairs, these great laws of right, which we name laws of justice, truth, or honor, belong to the mutual law of love. It is the great law of human attraction. It binds man to man and man to God. To use the modern language, the forces of these laws are correlative. And as I find that electricity and magnetism are the same, and then that electricity can be born from heat, or heat can be born from electricity, that the two are co-related or correlative, so I find that justice and love are co-related, that truth and love are co-related. I must not speak of the one without thinking of the other. When the Saviour said, in this text, "The Law hangeth on these commandments," he meant merely the law of Moses. But he did mean also, that the law in which we love God, and the law in which we love man, are one law; they are co-related. And in a hundred other words he showed that here is the principle of the law, not of Moses, but of all human life.

I do not go out on a day's duty merely with that hard resolve that I will measure so much work; that I will hew to such a line. I will not try to satisfy myself, by obeying such a statute, given at the State House, at the Capitol, or on Mount Sinai. No; my obedience is willing obedience. My service is perfect freedom. For what I call my duty is done because I love the Lord my God. And because I love Him, I love my neighbor as myself.

> "Father, I bless Thy name that I do live
> And in each motion am made rich with Thee.
>
> "May each new act my new allegiance prove,
> Till in Thy perfect love I live and move." [1]

---

[1] Jones Very's sonnet, "In Him We Trust."

THE CHRISTIAN MYSTICS.

"Seeing we are compassed about with so great a cloud of witnesses, let us lay aside every weight." HEBREWS xii. 1.

THE course of Saturday lectures is of more importance than the modest announcement shows.

The name *Mystic* deceives the hasty reader. It is supposed that mysticism means something mysterious, — that it is the same as mystery. Indeed, it is a misfortune that the two words begin with the same four letters.

But, in truth, as the word is used by the gentlemen who have arranged this course, lectures on the *Mystics* have nothing to do with mysteries, or with anything mysterious. In the language of science, any person who believes in the presence and power of an unseen God is called a mystic. Every mother who teaches her boy the Lord's prayer is a mystic. The boy is a mystic if he says his prayer with courage and conviction. And when these gentlemen prepare to instruct us about the mystics, they promise to take the lives of ten or twelve men and women, beginning with St. Paul and St. John, who have on the whole done the most to make the world believe that God is and is here, that He cares for you and me, and that we shall be and are helped, when we come to Him as little children come to their fathers and mothers.

About forty years ago, a friend of mine, a student in Germany, called upon the great scholar Frederick Tholuck, in Halle. He explained to Tholuck that he was a Unitarian minister in Massachusetts. "Oh, yes," said the great scholar, "I know the American Unitarians. They are mystics." The words showed how careful his reading of our works here. They showed that he knew the difference between our work and that of Priestley and the older English Unitarians. But I have amused myself, when I have asked what some of the old-time Boston Unitarian laymen would have said, had they known that the highest authority in the world had classed them all as mystics. Josiah Quincy, the president of the college; Jonathan Phillips, Colonel Perkins, the leaders in business in Boston; John Quincy Adams, Governor Lincoln, Mr. Webster, and the other men who led the community in politics,— these were all mystics of the deepest dye; for they all said their prayers with a distinct feeling that a living God heard them and meant to help them. And they all knew that this Real Presence of God was more important than any revelation in any book, on any tables of stone, or by any prophet. Knowing this, they were mystics, through and through. Yet no one of them had ever heard the word used in this way; and I suppose that each of these men, till he died, would have said:

"I am no mystic, sir: I am a matter-of-fact, practical Christian. I trust God, and I know He will pull me through."

When the gentlemen who announce this course tell us that they will give us the lives of the more distinguished mystics of the last nineteen centuries, they promise to us the biographies of the men and women who have been nearest to the standard of Jesus Christ. More than this, — and this, it seems to me, is the most interesting side of their work, — they promise us the lives of eight or ten people who have done the most to place the world where it is to-day. For the advance in Christian civilization, while it is due largely to the inventors, to the Franklins and Watts and other people who have known how to handle wire and steel, — is due at the bottom of things to the men who have kept in close touch with Almighty God, who have known Him, seen Him as the pure in heart see Him, heard His suggestions from day to day, and have made clear to the world His Real Presence. They are the men who have followed Jesus Christ directly, in saying that God is here and not in the seventh heaven; that God is now, just as much as He was with Moses on the side of Mount Sinai.

To proclaim that the kingdom of God is at hand, while most people think it is going to come next year, or five hundred years hence, is the pleasure and joy of these men. To proclaim that the reign of God is here, just as much as in some four-square city of gold and jasper, known by the name of Paradise, is their joy and victory.

Oddly enough, the visible and mechanical organization of the Christian Church has ten or twenty times, perhaps more, drawn away Christian people from this certainty of God's presence. It has happened, therefore, that ten or twenty times there has risen up some prophet who has laughed at the organizations, or frowned at them, or defied them, or ignored them. He has simply gone about the world saying just what Jesus said: "Here is God, and now is God, and the kingdom of God is at hand." And these prophets have changed the face of civilization in which they lived; so that the real history of civilization is more wrought in with the lives of these men than it is with the lives of such men as Faust who invented printing, or Watt who invented the steam-engine, or Franklin who taught us how to tame electricity.

Now, the gentlemen who are lecturing on Saturday afternoons propose to tell us something of the lives of these prophets. And exactly as the prophet Isaiah is a more interesting person than King Hezekiah, though King Hezekiah made a great deal more show in Jerusalem in the time of

Isaiah, exactly so is Francis of Assisi a more interesting person in the real history of civilization than is Leo X., though Leo X. made a great deal more show in his time. In the time when Richard the First, putting on a magnificent suit of plate-armor, rode on a handsome horse in Palestine against another prince named Saladin, he occupied a great deal more attention in the world than did a man with a black gown named Bernard, who lived in Europe a generation before, and was rated in his time somewhat as a president of a Western college is rated with us now. But as it has proved, the man in the black gown named Bernard of Clairvaux has had a great deal more to do with the development of the civilization which puts you and me into this church to-day, and which has built up the great Exposition at Chicago, than twenty Richards, or Geoffreys, or Raymonds, or Johns, or Thomas à Beckets could have had. It is very true that it is not very easy to get at the lines of the power of such prophets. The Saviour said very truly that no man knew how the spirit of God comes or how it goes. It is as Mr. Thomson and Mr. Edison and Mr. Houston, and all of them put together, cannot tell us how the underground currents of electricity go and come. But when I hear my friend talking, in his own voice, at the other end of the Chicago telephone, I know very well that somehow some power has passed between me and him. And when I see Western Europe a paradise, where Bernard of Clairvaux found it a den of thieves, I know that somehow and somewhere the spirit of God has operated to bring about that revolution. The more I work over the science of history, the more I find out that it was Bernard and such prophets as he who worked this miracle.

I proposed to myself last Sunday, when I read the notice of the lectures, to use the time I have this morning in briefly sketching the lives which are to be illustrated as the six lectures go on, with the hope that I might excite the curiosity of some of you so far that you would make the study which these lecturers propose, not only on Saturday afternoons, but in connection with your wider reading for the spring and summer. For undoubtedly the tendency of all our reading is to inquire about the outside of things. We are just like the Pharisees who told Jesus they would like to see some signs. We like to have pictures in the newspapers. We like to have representations of external phenomena. All our temptations are that way. It is, therefore, as I said, a good thing if a set of scholarly young men will make us face about, and look for a little at the deeper causes to which all invention, all manufacture, all art, and half of what we call science, owe their victories.

As the week has passed by, however, I have satisfied myself that I cannot do more than I have now done in trying to awaken interest in the course which is proposed at Channing Hall. And I will only try to give a single illustration this morning — rather tempted, if we get any chances, to recur to the same tempting themes again as the spring goes on. And this illustration shall be simply the warning against ecclesiasticism as such, which has, in so many combinations of history, robbed the advancing church of the victories which were just within her grasp. A set of well-meaning, mediocre men of talent and some outside education, step in and push the inspired men of genius aside, saying, "You have done your work admirably well, dear friends; go off and sing your swan-song and die. We will make a machine out of the interest which you have excited, and this machine shall last forever." Then they get their machine running; but nobody puts any oil on the working points; it begins to creak very badly; people are not satisfied with its work, and another prophet has to start up and perhaps break the whole old machine to pieces before he can quicken the life of people again. And again he is sent off himself, while another mediocre set of men of talent come in and try to repeat his work: another machine is built up; there is another set of rusty pistons and pivots and wheels, and the world goes through the same discipline once more.

The central lesson of lessons is in the life of the Saviour himself. He is the first idealist of all time.

He lives and moves and has his being in his God. He lives and moves and has his being in God so absolutely and entirely, that, at the end of two or three centuries, the machine-men, the men of talent, say, " Go to, he is God; let us worship him. It will be a great deal simpler than trying to bring this intangible, invisible spirit, who is in all the universe, into our lives and hearts and souls." Of the life of Jesus himself, the history is one and the same, from the beginning to the end. To ecclesiastics on the one side, — generally called Pharisees, Scribes, and Sadducees in the Bible, — and to politicians on the other, — sometimes called Herodians, and sometimes by other names, — he says just one thing: he says, " The Kingdom of God is at hand!" He says, " God is here, and while books are very good things, and laws are very good things, and it is all right, if you want to, to tithe mint and anise and cummin, do, for the very love of God, remember God first. Come to God in every moment, and let Him preside while you are blowing your trumpets, while you are marching in your processions, while you are paying tribute to Cæsar." Now, it is impossible to read church history without seeing how often and how sadly this commandment of His gets turned upside down.

I remember standing in the cathedral at Mayence, the first time I had ever been in one of the great Catholic cathedrals of Europe, and doing my very best to come into sympathy with the service there. I have never forgotten the agonized expression of the poor priest before me, whose business it was in one hour to repeat the Lord's Prayer thirty-five times.[1] Just think of it! It was his duty to charge those words full with fresh and genuine meaning, as of a tired child sobbing in its mother's arms, thirty-five times as those sixty minutes went by. Take that as an illustration of what it is to be told, by the mechanical combinations of hundreds of years, by a long line of officers above you and behind you, that to draw near to God, in that particular hour, — three o'clock Sunday afternoon, on the 11th of October, — you must say those hundred or two words over thirty-five times. You see how entirely the thing, the ritual, comes to be first; and you make as a secondary matter the living, loving presence of this Holy Spirit, who makes worlds and sets worlds moving, shines in suns, opens blossoms, and ripens the fruit. And you may see just this danger in all the visible arrangements which we make so carefully for service and for worship. Now, Jesus Christ saw all this in its bald horror. Simply, he hated it; and he said very hard things about it. They wanted him, on the morning of the Sabbath, to say to a poor epileptic boy that he could not attend to him that day because it was God's Sabbath, that he might come to-morrow. The very care that they would

---

[1] The service is called a Triginta.

give to an ox or a mule who had stumbled into a pit, they would not give to a child of Abraham. And for such madnesses as theirs he scored them down pitilessly. No wonder that they hated him. No wonder that they wanted to club him and stone him and drive him out of the synagogue there in Nazareth. No wonder that they arrested him at night by Kedron, took him round to Pilate's judgment hall, lied about him and his purpose, and nailed him to the cross. Your man of ability, your man of talent, your man of machinery, revolts against the presence of the living prophet, who testifies of that which he has seen, and tells that which he knows, who brings in this flow of infinite life, sweeping down the valley of the river, and carrying away all the petty monuments of mortal ingenuity. The priest is apt to hate the prophet, and to nail him to the cross if he can catch him at disadvantage. He did so then.

Here is the account, in few words, of the failure of religion in history to do what men expect from it, and have a right to ask from it. Religion is driven away, and what Dr. Hedge used to call religiosity takes the place of it. You have a son of God, well beloved, going in the night to commune with God, and by day seeking and following His present law. You pay him all sorts of reverence. You build temples in his honor. You sing anthems to him. You worship him. But in the place he filled you do not find what you seek,—

sons of God who are trying in every moment to commune with Him? You have another set of Scribes and Pharisees. They come so far that they tell you that they, and not God, will make your laws for you. They tell you that God has given to them the management of your government. They even tell you that once a month you must come to one of them and tell him your sins and that he will tell you what to do about them. For fear you shall pray wrong, they write down your prayers for you. And so the children of God, who all happily at home, running to him for direction, walking with him, talking with him, doing what he bade them, and telling him all their needs, find in the course of a few generations that they have all been shipped off to a far-away boarding-school, where teachers are very highly recommended by other people like them, but where, alas! they are very homesick. They do not see the Father's face, and they are all the more apt not to do His will. It is thus that the sweep and progress of religion, from which you had hoped so much, falters, stops like a vessel which has missed stays, quivering in the wind, and losing all progress. And it is then that Augustine cries out:

"Oh, my God! I could not be wert Thou not in me, or unless I were in thee."

It is then that St. Francis takes me out from the cloister into the world, and the very chatter and singing of his little birds teach me how God loves His creatures and His children.

It is then that George Fox warns me that every word must be simple, my manners and daily life cut loose from things, while I listen to the present Spirit of Life,— a Spirit who is He, and not It, — a present God, and not an ancient Law. It is in such a crisis that Channing comes, and in the midst of his intellectual triumphs we hear him whispering to God, "O God, give us a deeper sense of Thy presence, and instruct us to devotion by every scene of nature and every event of life." And so, a generation later, in our own time, Waldo Emerson, the spiritual child of Channing, wakes this whole America of ours from the formalism of its ritual and the rigmarole of its creeds, by going and coming, singing and preaching, at the fireside and on the platform, teaching the immanent presence of God. "This is God who tells you what is right. He is God who makes the world so beautiful. He is God who will carry the nation through. Why are you troubled when you have the living God to fall back upon?"

"And we, seeing we are girt about by so great a cloud of witnesses;" we, who come here one day in seven, lest the dust and smoke should separate us from God; we, though we have not idols to break nor parchment creeds to trample under foot, — we may well ask if we are God's children, or only His servants. He speaks to me if I will hear, as to Isaiah or to St. Francis or to Channing. This clear voice of Right, — do this, do that; right hand now, left hand now; ah, it is His voice. It is His present love. It is no decision cut on an old mossy stone for Hebrews or Phnœicians. This heaven of blue, this wonder of the snow, this glory of starlight, it is He who spreads it for me to-day. Father dear, I am grateful! To-day we hear His voice; to-day we can do His will; to-day we can rest ourselves, tired children, in His arms.

FAILURE AND STRENGTH.

" Why could not we cast him out? "
MARK ix. 28.

THE incident is fairly pathetic, whether we consider the Saviour's part in it or theirs.

He has determined on a great plan which has since succeeded, — a plan then wholly new, of lifting up this world. This is to be done by sending out into it twelve men who believe in God, and rely on Him. They are to make other men believe in the present reign of God. And these others are to make others try it.

Now comes a little local experiment on this plan. The Master is away for a little while, perhaps for a day or two. He comes back to the little company, and everything has stopped short. Things seemed hopeful and cheerful and to be advancing when he went away; and now nothing is cheerful, nothing is hopeful, and nothing is advancing. Nine of the twelve have been left to show what they can do, and they can do nothing. This epileptic boy has been brought to them, who would have been soothed in a moment had the Master spoken ten kind words to him; and they have not the spell. Whatever they have spoken has done no good. They cannot cast out the devil. And to the Master, as he comes, their confession is simply the confession of failure.

The whole story is so exactly like experiences of our own, that, as I said, it is indeed pathetic. How often do we see people who have been eager to be placed in positions of command, who are wholly unfit for those positions when the moment comes. In Mr. Adams's very entertaining history of the United States, with all his own humor he describes this position of the commander-in-chief of the American army at the beginning of the second war with England. Everybody has been boasting about the taking of Canada: we were to take Canada within the first four months after war was declared; it was in every speech that we were to take Canada; Canada was to fall into our hands like a ripened pear from a tree. And now here is the commander-in-chief who is going to do the taking, and the critical moment comes, and he knows no more about the taking of Canada than you or I do about the calculating of the curve of a comet. For a few weeks he continues this refrain, that he is going to take Canada; after a few weeks he becomes more silent on the subject; and, when five or six months have gone by, he says to the President that if he wants to employ him any longer he may, but that for his part he should be glad to retire to private life. He finds that it is one thing to suppose one's self in a place of responsibility, and another thing to be in that place. This is just what the nine apostles found. It is what Judas Iscariot, the traitor, perhaps suspected. It is the same as Thomas, the inquiring sceptic, finds. They are here with a world to save, and they cannot save it.

The moment the Master arrives on the scene, all is well again. The little encampment, if it were an encampment, takes on light and life, and begins to look forward and not back. The sick boy goes happily home with his father; the visit has answered the purpose. The people around feel that there is somebody who has power, and they recognize his authority. And things seem as they seemed before he went away. And then it is that these poor fellows, who have failed so absolutely when for the first time they were intrusted with responsibility, come and ask Jesus what the matter was, why they failed as they did fail. And he makes to them the answer, which to one and another he has made so often, "It is because you had no faith." "If you had faith as a grain of mustard-seed — why, think what a grain of mustard-seed comes to. It obeys the laws of its being; it accepts the infinite life which is offered to it all around; it grows and becomes a tree; a million other mustard-seeds are planted from it; and in the end their shade envelops the earth." He leads them to look forward, as he always does, and to look outside themselves, as he always does. There is victory secured, if only they will accept for their own the infinite law of all nature and of all being, and will not try to work their wonders by their own poor, broken little wills.

And this is exactly what he says, or what his Father and our Father says, to us, at any moment of our discouragement: "Why art thou cast down, O my soul, and why art thou disquieted within me? Hope thou in God, for I shall yet praise him who is the help of my countenance and my God." You are cast down, you are discouraged; because of your own devising and your own purpose you are expecting to work the marvels, you are expecting to cure him who is sick, or to bind up that which is broken, or to bridge the chasm which is before you. But this is not the way any marvel is to be worked: it is not by our power, but by infinite power. The chasm is to be bridged, not by our wit or wisdom, but by infinite law. You have failed, because all alone you have attempted the duty that was before you. You would have succeeded if you had acted in the infinite harmony, if you had availed yourself of almighty law, knowing, indeed, that you were acting in the divine and almighty purpose.

All this I am saying, as I promised I would, some weeks ago, when I was speaking here of the daily conduct of life. Even from hour to hour, between the moment when we rise in the morning and the moment when we close our eyes in sleep after our evening prayer, there are two distinct lines of life on which one may make his daily plans, may fight the battle through, and may write his journal of victory or failure when the thing is over.

I may arrange my day as if I were the centre of the universe. "Look out for Number 1" is the proverb of such a life. A great deal of introspective religion — of the religion of repentance, and reward, and punishment, of convent and cloister — looks this way. Many well-meaning books on what is called self-culture look this way.

Or, from the view of the universe, — the view God takes, for instance, — you may look upon your life. A good illustration is the view which an intelligent private soldier has of a great battle, if he is so placed that he can see, say, the steadfast firmness of the centre, the rapid dash of the cavalry on the extreme right, the precision of the shots of the artillery on the extreme left. Such a man comprehends something of the exigency of the day. He does his own part, not that he may be paid next pay-day, or that he may have two biscuits for supper to-night, but that the army may succeed; and for his country, that peace follow war.

In the first point of view, the very highest life one rises to is to pray, " O God, save my soul, and lift me into heaven."

In the second point of view, one rises to the spirit of all the hopes and petitions of the Lord's Prayer. In this point of view he says, " Thy kingdom come, Thy will be done on earth as it is in heaven." And then one remembers that one's daily bread comes from the co-operation of a million brothers and sisters. And as one asks forgiveness, one remembers those who have crossed his path unkindly; so his prayer goes on with forgiveness for them.

The first point of view states everything in the singular number, "I and me and mine and myself." It deals with finite and limited relations.

The second uses the plural number, and deals with the infinite relations, Heaven, God, the Holy Spirit, immortality, and the universe.

The adventurer whose daily life I began to describe here some weeks since may start away from home on one of these two lines or the other.

If he take the first, from choice or from habit, he comes to his office after his morning walk to say: "The walking is villanous to-day. The people are very much to blame that they have not opened the gutters. I went above my boots a dozen times, and now I must dress again."

If he have taken the other line, it is to say: "The day is marvellous for beauty. The sun has all his old power, and the snow is melting everywhere. The lumbermen in Maine will be delighted. There is no fear of short water at the mills. There is a set of fine fellows cleaning out

Tremont street, and I stood five minutes watching their work, and wondering that so much science could be put into such humble duty."

And at the end of the day the entries in one's diary differ, in like wise.

If he have chosen the individual or personal point of view he writes: "Tired to death and a good deal disappointed. I was just too late for John, because of a block in the street. I missed James, and I suppose he forgot me;" and so on.

If he started on the other line he writes: "There is good news from Washington, where we have hopes of carrying the bill. The 'Cephalonia' has a good day to start, and I found the Joneses all in good spirits at leaving."

In our modern language we say that one of these people is low-toned, and that the other is always in good spirits. The probability is that the Saviour's language is more accurate. If either of them asked him about it, he would say on the first case, "You need more faith." To the other he would have said that he understood the law of the grain of mustard seed, because he used what faith he had.

What is this essential Faith? I hope it is useless to say that such faith as is thus illustrated is not such arbitrary acceptance of four or five facts as can be stated in a verbal creed. A man might say truly, as he started on the day, "I believe in

God, the Father Almighty, and in Jesus Christ, his Son," and yet might go to his daily duty on the first of my two lines. And the same man would be quite unconscious, when, in the afternoon, he looked in at the Lenten Service and said the same thing, that such belief had anything to do with his dissatisfaction of the morning. All the same it is true, as the Saviour says from the beginning to the end of the Gospel, that that man wants more *faith*.

It is not that he wants to assent to more propositions of history or science: it is that he wants to rely on the foundations of life. In truth, he has been relying on its superficial phases. The Hebrew word which we translate "faith" in the Old Testament expressed this. Where David and the prophets are made to talk of faith, they really said, "foundation" or "rock;" and Jesus alluded to the same thing when he speaks of the man who builds on a rock, and when he says his church is to be built upon a rock. He means that, beneath all talk of "me" and "my," beneath all forms and frivolity of external life, there is one great reality named God, there is one infinite life called Heaven. And he means that people who have faith live in absolute relations with God, and live consciously or unconsciously in this present heaven. Of course, in such a life, my friend in his daily affairs does not distress himself so much about the condition of the sidewalk; for his mind and heart and soul are engaged more with the grandeur of the realities of heaven. As an old officer said to me the other night, " Phillips Brooks never thought of himself at all, and so he had more time than most men to think of the rest of the world and of God." This was a shorthand and convenient way of putting the contrast.

And we see that just the same thing is shown when we compare these apostles who wanted to cure this boy by a certain method which could be written down in a book, and the Saviour, whose constant communion with God and habit of living in heaven gave him, of course, the strength, the tenderness, and so the command, to which the poor sick boy yielded at once, and could not help yielding. Just that same contrast, as we shall find in every-day nineteenth-century experience, may be wrought out as you and I come and go.

Rely on the Realities. This is the direction of the Saviour, and every leader of men from that time down has proved its truth. The realities are God, heaven, and the solidarity of mankind. For you and me he promises success to those who will try the great experiment of such reliance. I shall conquer my low spirits, he says, if I forget them. I shall forget them if I do as he did, — if I follow him; if I pull this ox out of his pit; if I lead that blind man a mile or two on his way; if I write a letter to his sweetheart for the Italian beggar; if I find a home for the woman from Syro-Phœnicia, whom I find on Oneida street, puzzled about her English verbs, and chilled by the drabble of a north-easter.

I shall go cheerfully to my work, he says, if I will start on it as an archangel would. Take it as God's work, and God will put it through. It is God who teaches the acids to act on the alkalis. It is He who drives the electric current through the trolley. It is He who long since packed away His sunshine in what is to-day my coal, and He and I are succeeding together, as I build my fire on what is His hearthstone and mine this morning. A simple statement, and one which I find convenient when I am bored or in any way worried, is, that He wants me to make my life as large as His, and that it is really my blunder if I do not. And that is certainly what the Saviour means when he says it is God's kingdom in which I live, that the kingdom of God is at hand. Let a man sort out his day's errands, as George Herbert swept his floor, making God the cause and motive, and they cease to be annoying as they range themselves about infinite affairs. The breakfast or the supper which I eat becomes the answer to my daily prayer for daily bread. If I take them so, perhaps with the thought of some Sunday of communion; or if, as I break the bread at the home table or fill the cups, I see that God has ordered the world that I might fill the cup or break the bread, — I shall be less critical about flavor, or the accidents of my own taste. It is for me that Columbus sailed and Da

Gama doubled the cape of storms. It is for me that Stephenson built his engine, and Fulton started the "Clermont." It is for me that the chemists have grappled with silent Nature and compelled her to speak; for me that the mines give up their treasures, that the smiths gave form to metal, and the seamen crossed oceans to carry hither and thither what they did. I say in my prayer, "Give us this day the bread of our being." I sit at the table and I see how the world of God's children are made to answer it, in His care of a world, which is one world, and not a bag of pebbles. I eat and drink there, as Raphael ate and drank when he supped with Adam. It is not as a hog might find an acorn of whose history he could know nothing, and munch it, greedily, but with complaint, as he went to look for another.

This season of depression of spirits, which took the name of Lent, forced itself upon the church in the northern hemisphere, because in the short days of a northern winter, in its imprisonment and frequent lack of food, the body of man grows weaker, and he cannot do as he would. Is the spirit willing? The flesh is weak. In southern latitudes, if they retain the annual ceremony, they will have to change the months to September and October, when winter is ending. It is in such weakness and discouragement that men and women come to the Father to acknowledge failure. "I am ill-tempered, Father," or "I am discouraged," or "I cannot see as I would," or "I do not hear," or "I am horribly lonely in the world," or "I never succeed in anything with success." It is — as with the apostles — this devil or that devil whom I cannot cast out. "Why cannot we cast them out?" And the answer is always the same: "Dear children, you must stand on the rock. You must rely on the realities. Live in the Spirit, walk in the Spirit, and you shall tread on serpents and scorpions, and nothing shall by any means hurt you. Draw near to God and He will draw near to you. You shall never be alone. Live for the universe, and you shall forget yourself, and gnaw at your heart no more. Accept that universe, and float on the constant current of its love, and your personal grief and your separate misfortunes are forgotten."

Why, there was a poor woman once who had only a cupful of yeast. But it was alive, and she trusted the infinite Law of Life. She hid it in the meal, and the life passed from one tiny grain into another. She set aside a little to be the mother of more yeast, and more, — and from that grew more and more. And it was all alive. And from the bread of that baking the world was fed, as from the trees from one mustard-seed its parched deserts were shaded.

PALM SUNDAY AND EASTER.

I.

PALM SUNDAY.

PALM SUNDAY and Easter Sunday,— contrast the two forms of victory.

On Palm Sunday you have what the world likes, what the newspapers like, what history likes: a multitude of people,— numbers always are popular,— the waving of palm branches, the clothes spread in the way, the cry of " Hosanna." It is what that lowest form of language known in our time calls " a success."

On Easter Sunday three or four women, dazed and wondering, come to Simon Peter and to the young man John, who are hiding in terror. They say beneath their breath, " He is not dead; he is alive."

Even a Philistine world, like ours, acknowledges that the triumph of Easter, in nineteen centuries, has been worth more than the triumph of Palms.

Was there, perhaps, a little preparation in advance of the triumph of Palms? Did Peter and Andrew, fresh from the Transfiguration, go up and down the road a little the day before, and suggest to this and that gay company of pilgrims, that it would be a good time at last for a little public manifestation? Were they a little tired of this indifference of the Master? Did they think it as well to force his hand, to compel him to assert his position? And was the humble triumph of the slope of Olivet the result of this little combination?

I do not know. Such things do happen sometimes, in excellent causes. I do know that the people shouted, " Hosanna!" that the people of Jerusalem shouted, " Hosanna!" and I know that the next Friday the same people, or some of them, cried, " Crucify him! Crucify him!"

Palm Sunday will teach us its lesson, and will make some preparation for Passion Week, if from our own times, modern as we think them, we trace the same contrast between the successes wrought by shouting crowds, and the success of the lesson taught by the women at the tomb. The success heralded by the newspaper, and the real successes of real life! They are always contrasting themselves against each other.

History is never tired of the contrast. She is pitiless in repeating it. There are thousands of elegant medals in the cabinets — silver and gold, very likely — struck to commemorate this victory or that, perhaps this pageant or that, where men who study the medal say that the pageant and the victory will not be remembered. People cannot tell now what the victory was. Here is Fame, with a trumpet, flying over a battle-field, — I can see that. And here are some letters and dates in Latin, — I can read them. But what do the abbreviations stand for, and where was the battle, and why was it, and when? Just there the medal fails. It is, indeed, one of the curious fatalities of pageants that the people engaged in them think so much of the drapery and the line of procession that they do not remember, as would be well, what the procession is for and why the drapery is flying. On the day when Boston was two hundred and fifty years old, I had the great pleasure, and I will say advantage, of marching in the procession which tried to fix on our memories something of the history of the past and of hope for the future. I was fifty-eight years old, and so it was easy for me to remember where I sat on the brick wall of the Granary Burying-Ground to see the procession of half a century before pass by. The recollection set me to inquiring of one and another old Boston man how much he remembered of the other great pageant in which the end of the second century was commemorated. It was almost the beginning of our modern centennial celebrations. There was no centennial celebration in 1730. I found no person who had any recollection of the event. Josiah Quincy in his prime had delivered an oration in the Old South: no man recollected a word of it. Charles Sprague in his prime had delivered a poem: one or two lines of the poem had strayed into use as quotations, but no man and no woman remembered that the poem was a part of the pageant. Indeed, so far as I could find in quite wide inquiry, the only recollection of the great ceremony, to which the city of Boston had devoted its best power and to which it had given a day, was the memory of a little boy sitting on the wall of a burying-ground, to see a regiment of soldiers pass by.

For this there need be made no complaint; it is as it should be. The procession, the bands of music, the banners, the palms of Palm Sunday, and the shouting of Hosannas, are as purely superficial as the foam on the wave of a beach. Another tide rises, and the marks which the foam has wrought upon the sand are gone. There is no reason for complaining that we forget such things. But there is reason for asking what there is which abides and continues forever, what there is beneath ceremony and procession. What was there in Jerusalem which was of more worth than bells and trumpets? If Palm Sunday were a Sunday which left no eternal word behind it, what was the eternal word which should be proclaimed upon some other Sunday?

I think we might put this question to ourselves of our own early experiences; we should always get the same answer. Here is a cheerful, brave woman, whose outlook on life, is far-reaching, who takes each day as one more opportunity for loyal living,—that is, for serving God and the people around her. You look on her with admiration; you see she has met the problems and solved them; she has wrestled with this and that angel, and no angel has gone by but has blessed her. Put to her your question; ask her to go back to recollect the great party which her mother gave the year she was to be received into the best society of her sex. There was all the preparation for the dress in which she was to " come out," there were all the gifts of flowers from her friends, there was the anxiety lest there should be a storm on the day selected. Happily the skies were clear; the great event was celebrated even by the clouds of heaven, which kept away; and the moon and the stars shone brightly down upon the pavement as her guests came in. The music was just what it should be; the most charming people in the circle of the town were there to welcome this new life, which was really not simply to take part in the enjoyments of the town, but was to be a real help in the administration of its social order. Yes, the function was a great function, and all passed by successfully; the letters which the different girls wrote to the different parts of the world announced that Mary's coming-out party was entirely successful.

But if you ask Mary to-day what it is which has told in the make-up of her life, and how it is that you find her to-day even and well-balanced, whether the news of the day be grievous or be joyful, she will tell you that it was not at the party that she began to live. She began to live in those quiet, long days, when the curtains were drawn down and no one came into her room; when her new-born baby child, almost too small to cry aloud, lay sleeping in its cradle by her side. It was then and there, as she thanked God for him and for her own life, that she wrought out the problems, that she saw the visions, and her life became eternal.

The man whose presence at a syndicate prophesies success to the enterprise which they have in hand; the man who has only to go to a preliminary meeting, and men are sure that success waits upon their banners because he comes, — is the same man whom you and I saw, fifteen years ago, as he made his bow to the president in Sanders Theatre, at Cambridge, and received the diploma which the college gave him. The newspapers of the next morning said kind things about the grace and vivacity of his Commencement part; twenty kind letters from old friends of his father came in the next morning to congratulate him that he was walking in his father's steps. The young fellow himself said, "This is indeed the Commencement of life. It is here and now that I take the oar with my unblistered hands, that I begin to take my part as one of the crew." But time has gone on; ask him, as you walk home from the syndicate, which was the real critical moment of his life. Ask him when it was that real success began. And it is absolutely certain that he will not go back to the festival. He has forgotten all about Commencement Day; he has forgotten about all the letters of congratulation. He will tell you of some lonely vigil by the bedside of a friend; or of some midnight ride in the midst of tempest, he alone with his God, when he heard the divine voice. God spoke to him and he answered; or he spoke first to God and God answered. It is in that moment — a moment, perhaps, like that of Easter morning, when the darkness is just giving way to gray twilight — that his real life began.

Of the Saviour himself the noblest record is that "he made himself of no reputation." Have Peter and John arranged this little triumph? He shows what he thinks of it by riding on an ass. Thus is it that the King of Peace rides into his capital. The stable has been the palace of this prince, the manger has been his royal cradle, and its straw his purple! First and last he has been teaching them the folly of human triumphs, in language and in deed which are pitiless. The multitude throng him; he sends them away. A miracle astonishes them; they shall not make it known. They offer him a crown; he goes off into a desert. This devil and that, from the beginning down, will make him, in the devil's way, "king of all the earth." But their ways are not his ways. Their triumphs are not his. Alas for any professed proclaimer of his kingdom, who asks by stealth or in stupidity if somebody, somehow, will not advertise his proclamation! Is it not possible that some cornet band, or some banner on the wall, or some happy placard, may announce that the apostle is to preach or the prophet to prophesy? Pitiless his denunciation in advance of all such manufactured triumphs! Hopeless the fall, as from the temple pinnacle, of the fool who has been so tempted by the Devil!

It is indeed curious to observe the same distinction and contrast in the history of Passion week itself. For the first half of it, Palm Sunday, Monday, and Tuesday, is all spent in public, in what you might call public successes. It is in temple courts, in the streets of the city; it is in the presence of great multitudes. Then all the surroundings change. Wednesday is spent on the hillside of Olivet, in the most serious talk, but still private talk, with the Apostles. It is to them by themselves and not to any multitude that he tells how the Son of Man shall come in his glory. It is to them that the parables of the judgment are told. And with every evening, in that charming hospitality of Bethany, the great story gives its most distinct pictures of life at home. With the supper of Wednesday evening at Bethany, that day's history ends.

Then, as the most sympathetic critics have observed, such men as Keble and William Peabody, when we come to Thursday, even this record ceases. Thursday, the last day of his life, until the evening comes, is the one silent day of the Gospels. It is impossible to escape the suggestion that the talk of that last day, so eager as it must have been, was too personal to be written down. It was Matthew's confession of weakness and his personal suggestion of strength; or it was Thomas's confession of doubt and his tender and certain solution. Or it was John's confession, made for the hundredth time, that his temper had broken down, and the word of encouragement and suggestion which held John up through manhood to age. Too personal and precious, observe, for Matthew or for John to write down. Too tender and personal to come into the traditional narrative of Mark or of Luke. So tender and personal that the seal of silence which shuts them will never be broken.

It would be no bad thing if in your Bibles, between that gorgeous imagery of the words he spoke on Olivet, when they saw the rays of Wednesday evening's sun flashing on the gilded pinnacles of the temple, — if between those words and the simple, serious story of the Lord's Supper on Thursday night, there were left a page of white paper. That white page might remind us of what we are perhaps too apt to forget. It might remind us that there are lessons too deep for words and which are not to be written. It ought to remind us that we are not to go out into the streets and ask what hero is hearing the loudest Hosannas. We are not to search the pavement to find where lie deepest the trampled leaves of forgotten palms. For it is in some secret chamber that the infinite whisper of life has been spoken. It was when the soul was alone with God that God gave the promised blessing. Or it was in the gray of a cold morning, when the night damp still hung over the earth, before the sun had risen, before the white of twilight was even dappled with the rose, — it was then and there that those weeping, wretched women received for all the world the certainty of the eternity of Life.

To-day is the beginning of the Christian year. The next Sunday is the great Sunday of the year. For you and me, as the year goes by, there will be thousands of lessons of the infinite life, — suggestions, encouragement, and warnings. What is most curious is, that we have not now the slightest idea how those lessons, how those warnings, will come to us; through whose lips, in what society, by what parable or illustration. All that we know is, that somehow or other the living God will teach the lesson, and if you or I be enough awake to our royal privileges, we shall accept it and profit by it. If not, not. The lesson will be wasted, as the music of the spheres is wasted in empty space where there are none to listen. Of those lessons not to be counted, not to be foreseen, lessons of the presence of God, of His love and of His power, the only thing certain is this: that they will not come by observation. We shall not hear them in the crowd, where the escort is gathering, the procession forming, and the marshals ordering its march. We shall not hear them where the trumpets are sounding, when the people are shouting, or the newspapers are prophesying.

Elijah sat waiting for his lesson in the opening of a cave in Horeb. And a tempest swept over the hills, filled the air with dust so that no man could see, tore from their roots the gnarled trees and whirled them into the valleys. And there was no lesson for Elijah. He sat in the door of the cave, and the rocks shook before him as he looked out. He saw the crags tumble from the cliffs; he heard them as they crashed into the hollows. And there was no lesson for Elijah. And fire came whirling across the dry hills; it caught the gnarled trees; it blazed from their dry foliage; it left a record of desolation. But there was no lesson for Elijah.

But after the fire there came a still small voice, and Elijah heard it. For he was a son of God, and he knew God's whisper when it came. He was born of God. He was a spark from the infinite fire; his breath was the infinite Life. And, when the Power who works for righteousness gave him his silent order, Elijah knew and he obeyed.

For you and me it is not once a year only, in

the gray of the dawn, that we shall hear that whisper. It is not, as I said, into the rush of throngs that we are to go to listen for it. It is to be, perhaps, at the moment of most oppressive sorrow. It is to be, perhaps, at the moment of most exquisite joy. It may be in answer to the most intricate doubt. It may be while life seems most strong and its purpose most clear. What is certain is, that the vision is there if we open our eyes to see. God's kiss of love is there if we will rest in His embrace. His lesson of life is there if we will listen when He whispers. "If ye seek me, surely ye shall find me, if ye seek for me with all your hearts."

"A roadway carpeted with palms and flowers,
A welcome shouted by the eager throng:
A thousand voices sing in David's song,
'Messiah comes, the nation's King and ours.'

"Shouts, songs, and palms! Yet as the week goes by
The shouts are silenced and the palms are dry,
Till that last day, when blackness shrouds the sky,
And those who shouted then, to-day cry, 'Crucify!'

"A cold dark morning, and a new-made tomb;
Three weeping women groping through the gloom,
To dress a corpse from which the life has gone.
'And who shall roll away for us the stone?'

"Only one streak of twilight, cold and gray,
Whitens the east and gives a hope of day;
But see, it mounts the heaven, — 'The sun, the sun!'
See for the world *Eternal Life* begun."

II.

EASTER.

EIGHTEEN hundred and sixty years ago Jesus Christ and his twelve apostles were alone together in an upper chamber at Jerusalem. It was at the annual thanksgiving feast of their people. But for them the feast had all the seriousness of parting. He told them, and they began to see, that they met for the last time.

To-day that meeting together of theirs around that table is commemorated by a similar observance in hundreds of thousands of churches, formed by persons who take his name and call themselves his followers.

The day after that festival he was killed, — or the Roman centurion who was told to crucify him said so: and such people do not make mistakes. He was crucified and laid in a tomb. The apostles who had been round him, and their handful of companions, spent the next day in abject terror. And then night came, Sunday morning dawned, and that abject terror of theirs was at an end forever. The women of their company had been to the tomb, and his body was not there. Mary Magdalene had lingered there and had seen him. And that night, as they met in wonder, he came himself and spoke to them.

From that time forward they never believed in death.

From that time forward they led the world to believe in life, and life more abundantly.

And so it is that day which the new world celebrates as its birthday. About Adam or Prometheus, or the other stories of the beginning of physical life, it has no memories, — scarcely any legends, — certainly no birthdays. As to its real life, — its infinite eternal life, — it knows it began on that Easter morning.

I have said this real life, this infinite and eternal life, choosing those words, which are, however, rather weak, instead of the simple word " everlasting" life. The world has not, I believe, always drawn the distinction as to these words. Even in merely studying the history, we ought to see that those eleven apostles were wakened on Easter morning to a sense of what he meant by Life, which included much more than the idea of continued existence. From that time they had some sense of what he meant by abundant life; they knew what he meant when he spoke of the life of God. It is worth remark that in each of the great battles which he had with different leaders of the Jerusalem Jews, he tried to drive home this sense of what it is to live. Here they were, fussing over processions and trumpets and bells and ritual, and he speaks of everlasting life, of the light of life, of life more abundantly. And when he denounces them it is to say, " Ye will not come to me that ye might have life." Such words mean much more than the continuance of life beyond the grave. They mean life which has the power of the life of God. They mean that if these people will follow him, if they will enter into the dignity and majesty of his life, they will be as gods, creating, maintaining, determining, and so living in infinite life by infinite law. It is infinite life, life which is not to be bounded, — not simply prolonged life, life which extends in one direction. What he promises is not long life simply: it is large life, — life powerful because it shares the infinite power; life glad because it enters into infinite joy; life radiating on a million lines because it is knit up with the life of all other living beings. It means this, as well as life which looks forward to an unlimited future. And what these eleven apostles got a hint of on Easter morning was this reality of the power of life. It would break the tomb, — yes; but it would do more. It would denounce Tiberius, if Tiberius lived on any low plane. It would break up every superstition and ritual, unless the ritual had wrought itself in with the eternities of men's being. It would take every man outside himself, beyond his own headaches and heartaches, into the common life of the universe of the children of God. It would enable men really to partake of the divine nature, to use the strength of God when they were at work for God's purposes, to live and move and have their being in Him.

From one age to another, according as the

world is looking forward in its Christianity, or is only looking back, the real life of divine manhood reveals itself to the world or is shaded by black clouds. On the whole, what we may call the Church has not made a very rapid advance in extending the sense of the infinite power of human life. The world has relied in one century on the power of steam, in another on the power of armies, in many others on the power of lies; often on the power of close organizations of men. When it has relied on such things, it finds they all perish; and it has had many very bad set-backs. It is not difficult to imagine a personal devil, organizing the attacks made upon a stupid world, which has chosen thus to forget that its Master and Leader told it that it came to its full power only in the eternity and infinity of Life. It is easy to calculate that if the one little church at Jerusalem had been represented only by two churches in the world at the end of the first century, and these two only by four at the end of the second century, and these four only by eight at the end of the third, — if the Church had had confidence enough in its own great secret thus simply to double the number of its congregations as every century went by, — it is easy to calculate that there would be more congregations of men living in the divine life to-day than there really are congregations called Christians on any pretended roll of Christianity. This means that there have been years, in truth there have been centuries, in which the world is wholly satisfied with machinery, wholly satisfied with groping in archives and examining the entrails of mummies, and in which it is faithless and incredulous as to life and the miracles of life, as Thomas himself was.

Just in one of those black nights there steps into the world some new John the Baptist, who makes some men repent on their sins, who makes some men who are looking down into the dust look up into the heavens. And this man having prepared the way, some son of God, who is alive with the life of God, steps in after him, and he cries out, as Luther cried out, "You are alive if you know that God is and that you are His children." Or he cries out, as Wesley cried out, " Here is God, and now is God." He repeats the old lesson of the beginning, and the world comes up from its groping in the dust and stands awake upon its feet, and looks up to the heaven of God. It goes about the Father's business, as the Son of God well beloved did. And it begins to live. When this happens to the world, why, the miracle of Easter is renewed. And when this happens to the world, it makes one of the great advances which are the real advances in its history.

One cannot but ask, if he go beyond the forms of festivity, what will come to pass when the world shall take seriously the lesson of Easter? Not satisfied with flowers, and the sound of music, and congratulations that Christ is risen, what will take place when the world wakes from its own sleep, and rises itself? It throws off its grave-clothes, it rolls away the stone from the mouth of its tomb. It rises from death. It begins really to live in the eternal life.

What then?

A thousand million people — sons of God and His daughters — will begin on that Easter morning, wherever it shall come, to engage themselves in God's affairs first and in their own afterwards, and then only as their affairs relate to His: as in the rush of a great battle a brave soldier for a few moments forgets his own danger, even his own life, in the determination that the colors shall go forward, and a certain ridge be won. On such an Easter morning every one in Boston wakes, and starts on this day absolutely determined that every one in Boston shall live in a neat and cheerful house, with enough to eat and drink, and that wholesome and attractive; with clothing and fire to protect against cold and storm; with books and music and pictures of the best. So far as physical appliances go, every one in Boston highly determines that any one in Boston shall be thus befriended.

For the babies in Boston, for the boys and girls who are older, for young men and maidens, everybody in Boston on that Easter morning wakes determined that not one of them shall be led into temptation. On the other hand, they shall be prejudiced in favor of the realities of eternal life. They shall all be prejudiced in favor of telling the truth; they shall be prejudiced in favor of cleanliness and honor; they shall be prejudiced in favor of social life, and against morose or lonely life. As a recruit in an army is encouraged to vigor, and dash, and to put things through, every one of these young people shall be encouraged to generosity, to bear his brother's burdens, to rescue his brother from fire or water or in any danger. They shall be prejudiced, all of them, to live heartily and with spirit in the common life.

This seems to mean that with this new impulse to life, of this possible Easter morning, the soul of this man, the soul of that woman, — the souls of all men and women, all youths and maidens, all boys and girls, — shall start up and control their bodies and their minds. To-day, on the other hand, the body of a man and his mental machinery generally control his soul and keep it under. When of a sudden he acts from faith, or hope, or love, the three attributes of his soul, he sets it down himself as something exceptional. He is a little surprised that it all turns out so well. He is like Mr. Maxim when he has flown a hundred yards on his machine: he wonders if he is not dead; shakes himself to make sure he is not dead; thanks God he is not dead; but all the same goes about on foot, or does not go about at all, for two or three days before he renews his strange experiment.

What the world needs is that its prophets and its poets shall persuade it at last that the real master is the soul, and that the body and mind are the tools. Nay, the great experiment, when any man dares try it, makes him his own prophet, his own poet, if he show him that with perfect faith, with abiding hope and absolute love, he mounts superior to the flesh and makes it do his duty. He gives orders to the mind, and sways its rememberings and its arguings. Life controls the tools, and the treadle and the fly-wheel no longer keep the life down to the pace of their dead and mechanical movement.

It is no bad experiment for a man to try in his own life, when and how his failures have come from his neglecting or forgetting the great revelation of Easter. Life rules; life directs; life conquers. But a man forgets this and trusts, say, to machinery; and machinery breaks down. Or, he trusts to habit, custom, or fashion. But it proves that these have no life in them, and they break down. Thus you say the precedent was thus and so. But it proves that all life had died out of the precedent, and the precedent is good for nothing. This is what happens to all rituals which have outgrown their own generation. It is vain for you to tell me that the ritual was first-rate ritual in the fifteenth century, or the tenth, or the fifth. It is good for nothing now, unless there be in it now the life that was in it then. If not, not. The cocoon is only of use in a museum after the butterfly has gone. And whatever else the butterfly resembles, he does not resemble a cocoon.

To make this examination fairly, my question as to failure is, where was the deficiency in faith, where the deficiency in hope, and where the deficiency in love? These three are the eternal attributes, and they give us the tests as to how much eternal life subsists in our affairs. Did my endeavor lack in what these books call faith? That is to ask, was it only related to some three or four trifles, connected with myself, my wishes, my memories, my comfort, or was it all wrought in with infinite relations, with laws of the universe, with the Power which makes for righteousness? Could my purpose be fairly called an infinite purpose, or was it a purpose only of my own surroundings? These questions all ask how much or how little faith there was in that affair. And I must ask just the same questions as to time. How long and how well will my work stand? Has it any place in the next year, or in the next century? What has it to do with my life when this body shall have crumbled back to dust and ashes? This is to ask how far that infinite relation which Paul calls hope enters into my endeavor. And to be sure that I, and me, and mine, and myself are eliminated from this affair, that I am at work as partner in the universe, as God works with His power and on His plans. I must be sure how much love there is in my enterprise. Love is the word which these writers have chosen to express our conscious relation with all conscious beings. And if life is to be infinite, its motive power must express the sympathy of universal love.

Easter is Easter to me if new-born children, if opening crocus, if the triumph of music and the welcome of friends, teach me once more what it is to live. Not enough to eat and to drink and to sleep. That is not life. Not enough to plant seed, or to plough and harrow to prepare for planting, or to harvest and gather into barns. That is not life. Not enough to read, to remember and recollect, to arrange such knowledge in order. That is not life. But to do these things — yes, as God does them; to do these things, because they make a part of Heaven. Yes, to do these things, so that these who are right and left of me, these who are behind me and before me, may share my effort and live as I live. This is life eternal and abundant. This is the secret of life with which Easter has to do. The life of faith and hope and love.

> "'Tis a new life — thoughts move not as they did,
> With slow, uncertain steps across my mind.
> In thronging haste, fast pressing on, they bid
> The portals open to the viewless wind."

And that viewless wind — it is the Spirit of the Infinite God. The Power who makes for righteousness takes possession of my being. The Power who rules the world is pleased to quicken me and make me live. And I,— because I accept His gift, because I am not satisfied with faith or fancy,— I live and move and have my being in my God.

>   Wake me to-day,— dear Father, make me see
>   How great a thing this is, — to live in thee.
>   E'en at an open tomb the lesson give,
>   And show me, Father, what it is to live.

MANHOOD.

"Let us make man."
GENESIS i. 26.

IN any board of education I should be told that the great object of education is to carry out this purpose of the good God. In any adequate treatise on government I should be told the same thing.

> "What constitutes a State?
> Men who their duties know;
> Know their rights, and, knowing, dare maintain."

And certainly if I turned to the directors of the various churches, to the people who say they are the Church and that other people must obey and follow them, they would say that this is what churches are for — to make men. And probably they would add what this noble legend of Genesis adds: "We want to make men in God's image, after His likeness."

Is it not, then, rather pathetic, that, with all their endeavors, the people whose business it is to make men, turn out so few specimens of their successful manufacture?

When I stand, as I have stood lately, to look my last on the noble face of a noble man, I declare to you that for days I am haunted by the question, terrible indeed, — which yet I am going to put to you now, — why there are so few such? It seems ungracious to entertain that question. I cannot help that. It is a question too important to shut it off; too important for us even to pretend to ignore it. Why have we not more men that are men? "Give us men who are good for something" — this is the real appeal of every branch of business, of manufacture, of letters, of statesmanship, of life. It is hard enough to find an expert who knows about his own business; a chemist who is an adept in chemistry; a dyer who really knows what the art of dyeing is; an engine-driver who does not strain or wreck his engine. You see this whenever a board of trustees has a college president to choose. Much more when the President has a cabinet to appoint or a foreign minister to nominate.

You are aghast when you see what is the material which presents itself. But when you go farther, and ask not for an expert merely, not for a lawyer, or a chemist, or a diplomatist, but for a man, the penury and failure of our plans for making men reveal themselves more terribly. Then is it that you repeat the groan, Why are there so few men? And when one changes the sex, and for the work of women makes the same inquiry, the women come out no better. You find a plenty of people fussing over detail, who, as somebody says, cannot tell a small thing from a great one. But you ask eagerly, and nobody tells you, where are the women? Where is our steady supply, not exceptional, not a miracle, which shall give

"A perfect woman, nobly planned"?

SUCH are rather gloomy questions, whether in education, in politics, or in manufacture. We shall best approach a solution of such questions if we will ask, more seriously than people are apt to ask, what a man is, or what a woman is. For deep down here is the real difficulty. The educator does not know what he is driving at, or the manufacturer does not know what he wants. Many years ago, when I was much younger than I am now, there died a man who had been of a good deal of importance in our public affairs. As is the amiable custom of our modern life, a meeting of his associates in business was called to extol him. That was easily enough done, for he had been a man of broad views, of marvellous mental power, and, for some forms of intellectual work, he had won the admiration of all the younger men in his calling. Accordingly, a meeting of important persons was held in the capital of the State where he had lived, and all the journals printed their eulogies upon him. I fancy it was published in a handsome memorial volume.

When all this was over, I addressed a private note to one of the leaders of opinion in this country, who had joined in this testimonial, as it is called. I said to him, "Why did you let your meeting pass by without saying that your friend's life had been embittered and made worthless by his habits of intemperance? At the very moment when his country needed him the most, he was able to do nothing for his country because he could not be trusted to the temptations of the table in the city of Washington." I said, "You place me, and men like me, in the pulpit, and bid us tell young men to keep their bodies pure and control their appetites. And then, when a man dies who has not kept his body pure and has not controlled his appetite, you trumpet his name before those same young men, and hold him up as an object for their veneration and imitation."

My friend was not in the habit of receiving rebukes from me. As things go, I deserved rebuke from him ten times as often as I had a right to give it. But in this case he had nothing to say. He sent me a blank, humble apology for his silence on that critical occasion.

I tell the story now because, in an instance which fixed itself upon my memory early in life, it showed me how we go about praising this and that and another special achievement, but failing, even in our eulogies, to ask for true manhood, to ask for what is involved in a text like this, when the great God of heaven is supposed to say, "Let us make man." In that case we had a clever intellectual machine. I can really conceive that, as the ages pass, some Babbage of the future shall invent a machine which shall do something like what this person had done. And then we award him our praises, perhaps we build him our monuments in Mount Auburn, we print our memorial volumes, and we wear crape upon our arms, as if this creature had been a man.

It is easy enough to see where the temptation lies. The captain of a crew, or the director of a gymnasium, estimates the people who come under his eye by their muscle, or by their power of personal endurance, if you please. But he is comparatively indifferent as to their intellectual resources, so only they can drive the boat along or can catch the ball or can obey orders in a *mêlée*. That is the business in which such leaders are engaged, and they are quite right in forming their decision as they form it. Just so with the teacher in a school of metaphysics, or in a technical school, or in an art school. It is his business to tell us, in the art school, whether a pupil have a quick eye or a delicate sense of color; in the technical school, whether he have that divine instinct for invention, or that nicety of eye and hand, from which the great improvements are born; in the school of philosophy, whether he have the mental precision which will enable him rightly to discriminate as to the expression which is to be given in the delicate shades of statement of reasoning. But, in any such case, the leader or teacher ought to be careful to say to us, "I present to you an artist," or "I present to you an inventor," or "I present to you a metaphysician." It does not follow, because we have an artist, an inventor, or a metaphysician, that we have a man. Yet it is very apt to follow, as in that wretched instance which I have cited, that when this artist has won the admiration and gratitude of the world by the work of his pencil or his chisel, we join to give him the golden crown, where he does not deserve the golden crown. We place him upon our loftiest pedestal where he only deserves a lower place. For we ought to give our highest honor,—and, as this world becomes the kingdom of heaven, we shall give our highest honor,—not to the artist, not to the inventor, not to the metaphysician, but to the man.

Within the next three months our colleges will be sending out the results of their work. They will present to the world the best that they can do. What will the directors of these colleges themselves say as to their achievement? From Labrador to San Diego they will say, "We present to you these youths, who have acquired skill in Greek or Latin or mathematics, or in the study of nature, or in the study of history." Possibly they will say, "We present to you this or that young man, who has successfully led his crew in a boat-race or in a ball-match." But there will not be one of them, from one end of the country to another, which will say, "We present to you this youth, who can control his appetites and can govern his mind." That is to say, there is not one of them which will venture to say, on Commencement Day, "We present to you a man."[1]

I am not now discussing the much-abused science of education. But I will say in passing that, where I have seen teachers fail, it has been always because they have made a mistake here. The dancing-master invariably exaggerates the attention to his art. And it is only one teacher in a hundred who rises so much above the detail as to say that the special lessons in his own line make only a limited part of God's great business of education. But it is not fair to say this of teachers only. The same mistake is made by the president of a bank, who has selected some bright boy for the lowest stage in that business, simply because the lad is quick at figures, and who finds out, when the little serpent has grown to be a big one, that he is too skilful at figures, and that he has no conscience and no honor. The same mistake is made when you have promoted your bright West Point lieutenant, and forced him up through the

---

[1] All that Harvard College says, in presenting the bachelor's degree, is this: "We present to you these youths, whom we know to be fit for speaking in public as often as anybody shall call them to that duty." This is the best that has been achieved in a course of study covering four years, and prepared for in many more.

grades till he comes out some day in command at a critical point, and you find, alas! that while he is so skilful in the drill and knows so well how to manœuvre, he has no general view of the situation and is powerless for active purpose in war. How many young men have made the same mistake in choosing to marry this or that girl, because she was bright in repartee, or because the rose mingled fitly with the lily, to find, before married life had tested her by a week's adventure, that she was a fool. All such failures only show different forms of the mistake on which I am harping. We select our agents for this or that convenient detail of the moment, and we find too late that we have only a performer, and have not a man.

We are thrown back, then, to the definition of manhood. And perhaps it would be fair to say that churches and pulpits exist, that sermons are preached, and that people come together to hear them, simply that this definition may be enforced week by week, and that week by week we may learn what is a man. A man is not a finely formed or well-trained physical machine. Physical strength and health come from manhood, but they are not manhood. A man is not a well-adjusted, well-trained — shall I say well-oiled? — intellectual machine. Reasoning, imagination, memory, are good tools of manhood, but no one of these, nor all of them, can make a man. A man is a child of God.

No language is fine enough to make the full statement, but this is the best that has been tried. He is born from God and he goes back to God. "Spark from the divine fire," the poets are fond of saying. "Light from the divine light," that is one of the Bible expressions. "Dewdrop from the divine ocean," that is an image hinted at in the Bible. Man is a living soul. Perhaps I shall not do better than to take this phrase. This living soul has the business of controlling this body, making it strong and quick, active and pure. This living soul has the business of controlling this mind, making that to be strong and quick, active and pure. And it is only as this living soul asserts itself, will not be swayed by the body or by the mind, — it is only thus that you have a man. It is only thus that you have a woman. Those of you who have to do with machinery know instances upon instances where, in familiar language, the machine "runs away." The locomotive runs so fast on a down-grade that for the moment it escapes from the hand of the driver. The steam which is called the power is not the power; for it is crowded back on itself by the impetuous force which the downward grade has given. Precisely in the same way one sees intellectual action, where the vigor of a man's habit of reasoning or where the distinctness of his memory gets the control of his conscience, gets the control of his will, and conscience and will are ridden over by the mere force of the intellectual machine. And in every day, in every hour of every day, you see some poor wretch who has let a bodily appetite so overmaster him that, as Paul says, he does the thing that he does not want to do. He does what he knows he ought not to do. The body has become too strong for the soul, as on that downward grade the weight of the engine was too much for the steam. All these are instances where in the man the divine power has been lost. It is fair to say that the man has ceased to be a man, in the true interpretation of manhood. The man appears only where the soul masters the mind and the body. The man appears where the true will achieves its real purpose. The man appears where the purpose of God is carried out. As Paul says, in that noblest epigram of the New Testament, to will and to do God's good pleasure, here is the sign of the present God.

You stand at the open grave of a friend, and whether you analyze your feelings and thoughts or not, here is what gives them their drift. Did he rule his thought and rule his body, or did his body rule him, or his books rule him, or his memory? Was he the lord of his own going and coming, or was he the slave of his machinery and his traditions? And when, as you turn away from the grave, you are able to say, " Here was one who had infinite purpose, who knew the divine purpose, and for that purpose lived," then and then only are you able to say, " Here was a man."

One hears a great deal in our time of better education of the hand, that our boys may be able to drive a nail without bending it, and that our girls may be able to make an intelligible drawing of a flower. We hear a great deal of athletic education, that boy or girl may be able to walk twenty miles a day, and sleep all the better for it, and be all the fresher the next morning. We are training the eyes of the little children to a keener sense of color; we are training their hands and eyes together to a quicker sense of form. But I wish that we could always manage, in this mere sharpening the edge of the tool — for it is nothing more — to give boy or girl a deeper sense of who it is who is to use the tool; how great, how unmeasured, is the power of the *boy* or the *girl*. If we could lead along boy or girl from day to day in this sense of possible mastery, if we could really make them believe that in the temptations which are likely to befall them they can really tread on serpents and scorpions, and that nothing shall by any means hurt them, we should not so much mind if the edge of the tool were not of the very sharpest. When Daniel Boone made his forest home, he owed more to the strength of the blow by which he drove his axe, he owed more to the precision with which the axe alighted in its preordained place, than he owed to the sharpness of the tool. And these boys and girls of ours are to succeed or are to fail according as it is in the infinite power of the child of God which undertakes the duties of manhood or of womanhood.

The lesson cannot come for them too early, and for us it cannot come too often, nor are we ever too old to review it, — "I have infinite power." That is the lesson. "As God lives I will use it. I will not let this body, which is not infinite, hamper it; nor this mind, which is all woven in with the body. I, who am a child of God, will use the body and will use the mind."

This is the true lesson when a great man dies, or a great woman. Little people ask, in a little way, "How could she do what she did, or he?" The great teachers answer, "Of course she did it. She was a child of God; she could do what she chose. Of course he did. Sons of God do not stop, or turn backward from the plough." And any boy or girl who hears me, who will try the great experiment, has this victory open. "I control my body; it shall do what I command. I control my mind. It shall think things which are pure, which are lovely, which are of good report. It shall not think things which are base and mean and in any shape wrong." The boy who makes that determination of a son of God, and determines — puts an end to all other notion, — in that moment becomes a man. The girl who thus determines becomes a woman. These two, at least, of us all, get an answer to our question. "Let us make man in our image," said the good God of life not so long ago.

And here are two of his children who propose to join Him in that endeavor.

Let me read you what Mr. Calthrop has said:

> " Upon God's throne there is a seat for me.
>   My coming forth from Him hath left a space
>   Which none but I can fill.   One sacred place
> Is vacant till I come.   Father! from thee
>   When I descended, here to run my race,
> A void was left in thy paternal heart,
> Not to be filled while we are kept apart.
> Yea, though a thousand worlds demand thy care,
>   Though heaven's vast hosts thy changeless blessings win,
> Thy quick love flies to meet my slow-winged prayer,
> As if amid thy worlds I lived alone
>   In endless space; but Thou and I were there,
> And thou embraced me with a love as wild
> As a young mother bears toward her first-born child."

THE WILL OF GOD.

"Thy kingdom come. Thy will be done."
MATTHEW vi. 10.

WE repeat the wish every day in our prayers.

Life is worth very little unless we have a real hope that the wish will be fulfilled.

And there is great danger of failure if we do not know what we mean or say. Still more danger is there if we mean nothing when we offer the prayer, in form, so often.

I may suppose, may I not, that here we are none of us perplexed by the idolatry of the letter? We are not confused by figures of poetry. We do not pray that in our time a chariot may ride across the heavens, and that the Maker of the universe shall descend from it, and sit upon a throne, and call us to judgment. Such a probability is announced, perhaps not far from this place, at this moment. But it does not trouble us who are here.

No; the kingdom of God is not here merely,— it is not there. It is everywhere where the obstinacy of man, the obstinate child of God, does not stand out against it. As we see a block of ice for a minute withstand the flow of the stream from which it was born, our prayer is that such human obstinacy or other folly may not arrest any longer the reign of God. It is that His will may rule this earth as precisely as when, last week, it ordered the sun to be eclipsed at the hair's-breadth of time, or of eternity, which the students of His will had foretold. This kingdom, reign, or rule of God, when our prayer is fulfilled, is to be everywhere. As Jesus says, "It is to shine as one blaze of lightning shines, over the whole world."

The words "Thy will be done" were consecrated by the Saviour in that midnight prayer of Gethsemane. But he does not use them, nor mean us to use them, simply as the palsied assent to a will we cannot change. It is not the dead surrender of fatalism, all but dumb. It is the acknowledgment of our ignorance, that we cannot foresee infinite purposes. And it expresses our certainty of God's love that He does not willingly wound our hearts. For the future it pleads, as it would trust the world to better law than rules it now. That the time may come when God's will shall have hushed the rage of battle. The time shall come when God's will shall have ended man-made pestilence. The time shall come when there shall be no famine. The time shall come when, instead of hunger and thirst, instead of diphtheria and cholera, instead of murder and rapine, instead of fraud and theft and intrigue, God's will shall be done on earth as it is done in heaven.

Famine, diphtheria, cholera, murder, rapine, may now be permitted in God's law; but when He rules the earth, as He rules the heavens, they cease to be.

Now, in offering to Him this prayer, we find ourselves just as we find ourselves when we render any lesser petition. If I ask another man for help, of course he turns on me to ask what I am doing about it myself. An officer asks the commanding general for a reënforcement that he may storm such a position, and the commander gives him the reënforcement only when he is sure that the officer means to do something. A tradesman goes to a bank and asks for a discount, and he must submit to pretty close inquiry as to what he himself is going to do with the money, how he has handled the last money they lent him, and how his business is going forward. These are little instances, but they illustrate the great necessity as well as if they were larger. I do not go to Almighty God and ask Him that His kingdom may come and His will may be done, unless I propose to do something about it myself. I do not go, if I am not at work as hard as I can to set it forward. Certainly I do not go to Him if I have no idea of what His kingdom is and what His will is. I do not ask in the dark; I am not clamoring, like a man in prison, who shrieks out behind his bars and bolts that he wants to be let out. I know I am a partaker of the divine nature; and to this infinite power who rules this world I come, and ask what we two, He and I together, are to do, and how we are to do it. Virtually, I pledge myself to my share in the endeavor. I pray that God's kingdom may come, and I promise that I will myself do my best that it shall come. I pray that His will may be done, and in the prayer I pay at least my own contingent; I promise that my own will shall be in accord with His.

This means, then, some definite understanding of what God's kingdom is to be, and some definite conception of what God's will is. Here it is that, as I am always saying here, we do not get along at all in the higher lines of life, to consider which we come here, unless we let the imagination work cordially and well, so as to sketch out for us on the screen a vision of a better world than we live in now. No man has a right to pray that the kingdom shall come unless he has some idea, however faint, of what the kingdom is to be. And as I implied just now, no man has a right to say "Thy will be done," in a dumb, dead acquiescence in a power which he cannot resist. He must imply that he is doing his part that that will may be done. My child dies in scarlet fever, and I say, "God's will be done." But when I say it, I mean that, from that time forward, my life is consecrated to helping men of science, and to helping the authorities of the city, in trampling out the germs of an unnecessary disease. If I can help it, and if we can help it, God Almighty will certainly do his share,— other homes shall not be desolated and other families made wretched by human neglect and failure in that line at least. So far as we can bring our resources to bear, God's will shall be done. From such a high determination as that, our Seashore Home was born and grew up, now fifteen years ago; and so many tears have been stopped before they began to flow, and so many homes have been living and light, because of that high determination. And, on the other hand, the first question to be put to any low-toned man, diffident, anxious, and distressed, who cannot see into the cloud, and feels that the world is running backward,— the first question to be put to him is whether he have any picture in the least adequate of what the world shall be when God is the ruler of it, and when His kingdom comes. At the very least, he ought to be able to say what is the post to which he is assigned in this business; in his daily life, from January to December, what is the service that he is rendering, so that this Boston shall be more alive with God's life in the year 1894 than it was in the year 1892? What am I doing in my way, however small, to bring in that hoped-for kingdom?

One asks this question and answers it, gratefully remembering how much power there is behind him. Colonel Greely told me that when he and his men were starving and freezing in Smith's Sound, in that hardest duty of waiting, he could cheer them by nothing so well as to tell that the country was behind them. He would tell them that the United States was used to have its way; and that the United States, at that moment, was resolved on their rescue. More than this, and better, when I pray to the Power who makes for righteousness that His kingdom may come. There are checks and hindrances. But they are merely drawbacks of time. And He knows no time. He is used to have His way. His name is the All-Mighty. And I, when I really live that His kingdom may come, I ally myself to His all-mighty-ness.

> This soldier was not armed like those of old,
>   Whose heavy axes felled their heathen foe;
> Nor like the bands whom later days enrolled,
>   Whose breast-worn cross betrayed no cross below.
> . . . .
> No coat of mail or sacred robe he wore,
>   Yet went he forth with God's almighty power;
> He spoke the word whose will is ever done,
>   From day's first dawn till earth's remotest hour;
> And mountains melted from his presence down,
>   And hell, affrighted, fled before his crown.[1]

Any adequate conception, I may say any decent conception, of man's own place and duty in these lines would relieve our ordinary talk of some of its worst cant. Here comes an invasion of cholera, sweeping over Europe and threatening America. Such a city as Hamburg is caught and

---

[1] From a sonnet by Jones Very.

overwhelmed. Such a hot-bed of disease as the country round L'Orient becomes a nursery of new pestilence. Now, when such a catastrophe as that takes place, that is only wicked blasphemy in which we roll up our eyes and talk about the providence of God, and the inscrutable purposes of God. And it is apt to be mere hypocrisy when we say, "God's will be done." We know enough now to know that but for the folly, superstition, and what one may call madness, of thousands of ignorant and bigoted men and women, no such invasion would take place. We can point out the focus-points in the East where this disease, originating nobody knows how, is permitted to multiply itself with a horrible geometrical progression, so that then its tiny germs are sent roving over the world. The whole thing shows, from point to point, at different ganglia of the world's circulation, ignorance, stupidity, the absurdities of red tape, the madness of absolute government, the superstition of one set of people and the indifference of another. Science shows that we have no right to talk about the mysterious providence of the Almighty, and to say simply that we will resign ourselves to a law that is higher than our law. It is both blasphemy and hypocrisy to use such words.

There is equal blasphemy and hypocrisy when we use them in our own homes. So far as any intelligent conception of the purposes of God goes, our children come into the world with the same expectation of being, and with the same prospect of long life, as a young elm-tree, planted in the soil it loves, in some fertile meadow. If you please to say so, that elm-tree has a definite period of life; when it has lived to be three or four hundred years old, so far as we know the laws of vegetation, its aged limbs are not sufficient to resist the gale; it breaks to pieces, and it dies. So far as the elm-tree's being goes, here is the law of its being, — growth, strength for so many centuries, weakness, and fall. But this does not mean that some boy crossing the meadow, who wants a switch with which to drive his oxen, shall not take out his jack-knife and cut down the elm-tree when it is three years old. Very likely he does so, and future ages, who never heard of the boy, and cannot so much as curse him, will suffer for the loss of the glory of the elm-tree, because he needed a switch for his cattle-driving. In a case like that, future ages, if they have imagination enough to know what they have lost, have no right to throw upon God, or upon His general laws, the loss of their elm-tree. If it were of any importance that blame should be rightly assigned, as it is not, the blame falls on the whim of the boy who destroyed it.

Now, when I am told, either by the pulpit or in the newspaper, or in the cant of private talk, that that is a mysterious providence which has cut off a man in public life from his duties, just when the State needed him most; or a woman in private life from the charm of her home, just when her home needed her most, — I resent the imputation upon God. I have come to hate that phrase, "a mysterious providence." I think we are wiser when we recollect how much and how far human folly and human ignorance are responsible. I do not know, and I will not pretend to say, for instance, to whose folly and to whose ignorance the present epidemic of scarlet fever in this city, or the annual epidemic of diphtheria, is due. But I do say that that is a very short and poor use of language which refers such things primarily to the will of God. I say that, primarily, they ought to be referred to the carelessness, ignorance, folly, or laziness of man. And, knowing what we know of such lapses, such failures, — say in the case of cholera which I described just now, — it is wiser to determine, on the one side, that I will trust that Infinite Goodness which rules so clearly where man has no share, and that, when I meet with evil which I cannot explain, I will accept the probability that it may be referred to some such human folly and failure. At all events, for myself, I will highly determine that, so far as my power goes, I will be a fellow-workman together with God, and that He and I will work together in the determination that His kingdom shall come.

I am not such a fool as to try, after seventy years of life, to solve the problem of evil. I can conceive of a world where the so-called man and woman should have no wills of their own, and be powerless to commit murder, to treat their children cruelly, or in any way to defy God's law. God could have compelled their obedience by law as accurate as that by which the apple falls or the moon eclipses the sun. But those creatures would not be men and women. They would not be God's children. They would be like billiard balls, knocked hither and thither, or they would be pebbles on the beach, rounded by the wave; but not men and women. God chose to give us, His children, the freedom we have. From that freedom comes your cholera, your scarlet fever, your murder and suicide. From it comes your bad government, bad drainage, bad water, bad streets. From it comes hatred, malice, and all uncharitableness. That is to say, visibly, and in forms easily calculated, nineteen-twentieths of human suffering and sorrow come from the meanness, duplicity, selfishness, and wickedness of men. It seems to me most unfair, and most illogical, that when we know this as we do, we should, for the other twentieth, which we cannot account for and which we do not understand, throw it upon what we call "a mysterious providence." Mystery enough; yes. But it is not fair for us to pretend, because we do not know how this has happened, that it is a blow of a Father's hand, who has devised this plan of punishment for our education.

"Thy will be done!" Yes. And, as in my tears and agony I say, "Thy will be done," I will recall what the prophets have sung, what the Saviour has promised, of that will when it does rule the world and make it heaven. One of these prophets saw the new heaven and the new earth, and the two were the same. The city in which men and women were to live was a new city, and it came, of course it came, "from God out of heaven." It was a holy city, alive with the thought of God, with the love of God. In that city, as he saw it, God dwells with men, and they know He does. If they walk, they walk with Him. When they sit at meat they talk with Him. And in that city, when He speaks they listen to Him. "He is with them and He is their God." It is not simply that they say He is one day in the week, and then are their own gods six days in seven. He is with them, and they with Him. Tears are there? Yes, at first. But He wipes them away. Death is no more in that city. Sorrow and crying are gone, and there is no more pain. This is what the prophet saw in a city which was really the tabernacle or home of God.

In that city, whether called the New Jerusalem or the New Boston, God's kingdom comes, and His will is done as it is done in heaven.

SUMMER SERVICE.

"He gave you from heaven rains and fruitful seasons, filling your hearts with food and gladness." ACTS xiv. 17.

SINCE we met here on Sunday I have spent more than half my life in the open air; much more than half of my conscious life. From 8.30 on Monday morning to 7.30 last night, I have been passing from place to place in Massachusetts, Connecticut, and Rhode Island, wondering at the lavish beauty of June, and in the delight of its sounds, its sights, its perfumes, its lights and shades. Insect, bird, fish, and beast, — here have been millions of living beings, who have either had the songs of Paradise to sing, morning and evening, or its still service to render, no less exquisite. Impossible not to join in that service, silent or vocal; and if one have been imprisoned for months, as you and I have been, in these prisons which we call homes, one joins in them with a certain intensity, which seems, perhaps, to one who lives in the midst of such marvels like the "provincial rawness" of the rustic when he finds himself in a city compacted together.

We are apt to say of every June — what is, I fancy, true — that it is more beautiful than ever.

True, because certainly man is more a child of God with every year than he was the year before. What we call inventions and discoveries, and what we call the improvements which spring from them, if they be real, are simply the finding out conscious Nature better than before, and the entering into the work of Nature and the Universe. This language, when interpreted from the conventionalism of science into the affectionate language of families, means that the child has found out the Infinite Father better, and has gone out with Him more fondly in his daily affairs. If Mr. Pope and his societies make for me better roads, if somebody contrives for me a better boat, if a wise Legislature opens up for me a wilderness, — so far, June is better for me, by mere physical improvement.

And if I, in the twelve months, finding my own card-castles fall, and my palaces of reeds blow away, — if I have determined to build on eternal foundations, to mount to the Mount of Vision, to accept no help but God's help, and no counsel but His counsel, why, by a law even higher do I come to take in the marvels of June more happily and certainly. If I become a creator with God, — if I have highly resolved to live, and move, and have my being in Him, I swing into the current of Infinite Life more joyfully. The song-sparrow does not sing to deaf ears, nor the arethusa open to blind eyes. So it is doubtless true, to the world at large, — let us hope to each of us, — that June is more beautiful with every year.

Wisely or not, we have so arranged our affairs in the matchless plenty and comfort of modern life, that, of the hard work of the world, nine-tenths shall be done in the months after the first of September and before the first of June. It follows that its play, its rest, its recreation, its vacation, come in June, July, and August. Even the wheat harvest of the West, which is to feed half the world, will be nearly all reaped before this next week is over.

The joy of exultant life which fills the communion-tables and altars of the church with flowers, on days of high festival, lifts men in worship and in religious aspiration wholly above that mean line which bids them bow their heads in the dust and cry, " Vile, vile ! "

Take our New England history. Puritanism found out in our own century that it had better work before it than compelling men to eat out their own hearts and brood over their two-and-sixpenny sins. It found that religion had to proclaim glad tidings to the world, and it organized its great missions. It found out that man must live with God, must enter into His joy — the child in his Father's business. As of necessity, the change showed itself in ritual. And our dear Dr. Andrew Peabody said that the first day a bunch of roses was placed on the pulpit of the South Parish church in Portsmouth might be called historical. Every newspaper in New England, he said, announced that there were roses in a church in Portsmouth. Our friend Charles Barnard used to say something like this of the flowers in Warren-Street chapel. I think that is one of their fair grounds for pride there, that they led the way for our decorous churches in this simplest observance by which we welcome the present work of the present God in what we call His most exquisite handiwork, if we dare discriminate. It is only a church which is trying to stereotype old-time functions, to make the prayers of the sixteenth century answer for the nineteenth, or the creeds of the eleventh answer for the twentieth, — it is only such a church which in symbolism can satisfy itself with artificial lilies, with violets painted on glass, or with roses carved in stone.

The true homage to conscious Nature is, in the language of religion, the glad worship of the present God. It is worship which I can render in the still night, on the deck of the ship, as God's stars point my way for me. Or I can render it far under ground in the shaft of a coal-mine, as my poor candle shows me how a million years ago God knew my needs and arranged for them. And never is such worship — or gratitude, shall I call it, or do you like the word "love" better — more simple and natural than when with all my heart I thank Him for the color of the forget-me-not, for the grace of the clematis, or the sweetness of my mignonette.

Scepticism has found, in our time, a coarse and hard reply to the statement that the firmament shows God's handiwork. "You must not say that because the world is, God is." This is the statement. "For if the world were not, you would not be, and you could not be arguing. This is what has happened to survive, under the law of selection, in which no one selects." But no such reply annoys me, no such doubt perplexes me when I have in my hand a spring anemone, or a sweet violet, or the lily of the field. The world could have existed without either of them. The great dice-box of destiny could have flung out its worlds into space, with no fragrant violet, with no wind-blown anemone, with no lily of the field, and the balance of gravitation would still have been perfect, the worlds would have rushed without fragrance and beauty wildly through space. When, in the same blossom, my eye here revels in color, when I find exquisite form and perfect grace as I enjoy the fragrance with the color and the form, you find it hard to persuade me that this is the survival of the fittest. When I find the dice always turn up triplets, I am sure that some conscious power loaded them. Whatever power made rose, and lily, and violet, and anemone, had the sense of beauty, and knew what my sense of beauty would be. So that when I find the exquisite Rhodora waiting for me in the wilderness, I say gladly, — it is my spontaneous thought — "the self-same Power that brought me here brought you."

I believe, what I do not pretend to prove, that that native joy came to me thus, because the Power that put the flowers here put me here, because His life is in all His works, and that His children, of whom I am one, come closer to Him as they know more and more of His handiwork, and enjoy what He enjoys; as they watch the present life in which His creatures live, and move, and have their being. I say, the present life in which they are now growing. God is. His name is I AM. It is not perhaps easy to think of Him as acting now, with just the thought and feeling with which the poet says He acted in the beginning, when God said, "Let the earth bring forth grass." But it ought not to be impossible.

God now says, "Let the earth bring forth grass." He *is* saying it at this instant, and because He *is* saying it at this instant, the earth *is* bringing forth grass at this instant; just the same creation *is* going forward now which, for convenience of language, we say *went* forward then, — in what, for convenience of language, we call the beginning. Perhaps one feels this present power of a present God a little more vividly when one sees it in an unaccustomed way. I have told the story here of one of our first men of science, of whom it would be fair to say that he experienced religion — though not for the first time, indeed — when he first put his eye to the eye-piece of a compound microscope of high power. In that moment he was a witness at least of the present work of God, seeing crystals shape themselves, seeing cells enlarge and double and separate; seeing growth in what seems to be its origin. In truth, there is nothing more remarkable when I see an atom, just now invisible, choose its conscious course, and work its way across a tiny drop, than there is when I see an eagle mount in the sky, poise himself in mid-heaven, and plunge in the deep below. In both cases I see an exertion of spontaneous will, and that is always unexplainable. But when I see this through the microscope, the sight shocks my dead habit, and I feel that God is now as He was in the beginning, and as He ever will be, world without end. "I AM is thy memorial still."

I grant the exceeding difficulty of thinking, feeling, believing, and seeing that God is a Spirit. I am afraid that difficulty will yet last for generations. The woman felt it at Sychar, when Jesus said, "God is a Spirit;" and her brothers and sisters have felt it ever since, and will continue to feel it for a long time. Even the language of the best books does not always help us. Thus the Bible language, and the hymns drawn from it, often run back to the child's notion, which was the earlier Jewish notion, that God lives in a particular place, that He waits for this message, and that He sends that angel. But in this great business which is central, everything makes one hopeful now. All science shows more and more one law in all space and in all time. Whatever Power made this world, the same Power who sustains it made and sustains Arcturus and Orion. To this Power there is no such limitation as space, there is no such limitation as time. Now, about this present Power you may have two notions. According as you have one notion or another, you may call it " it," and say, " It does not know what it is doing;" or you may call this power " He," and you may say, " He does know what He is doing." In this last case, you accept the religious philosophy of Jesus Christ. As you consider the lilies, you see in them the tokens of God's present love, and of His present wish that this world, among other worlds, may be beautiful and happy. To take Miss Fuller's phrase, which I used before, " You accept the universe." To take the quaint phrase of the Catechism, " You enjoy God." Best of all, perhaps, is the phrase of the parable, " You enter into the joy of your Lord."

I certainly am not going to argue in five minutes this great question, whether the Power which sustains this universe is He or is It; whether He be conscious of His work or not. Indeed, I do not think that question will ever be solved by argument. Rather, I believe, that a world of the conscious children of this God steadily moves forward and upward to its own solution of the question, and with every day, indeed, of the world's life knows Him more and knows Him better. "Nearer, my God, to Thee, nearer to Thee." In this great issue I like Dr. George Putnam's epigram, "You say that all this beauty, wisdom, tenderness, harmony, are the result of certain laws of matter, which you tell me are one law. I accept your conclusion. I believe what you say, only with a little change of language. If matter can do such wonders as these, wonders which in my highest spiritual flight I enjoy and prize, I find it better to call it Spirit. What you call Matter, I call Spirit." Or as matter of statement, I have found many people are helped by Freeman Clarke's simple statement, which I wish I could repeat in his own clear language. "You say that this exquisite human organization, in which a million million cells of being coöperate with each other for one aim, has resulted in the marvel of thought, in the marvel of conscious being, and in the greater marvels of Faith and Hope and Love. You tell me it is possible for a bit of mechanism to be so exquisitely perfect that the result is conscious Life; as if the beautiful organ yonder were so marvellously formed, that of itself, without direction, it should begin, when it chose, to play a symphony more marvellous than Beethoven ever dreamed of, and when it chose, should cease and be still. Very well, if mechanism can thus rise to consciousness in man, why may not the mechanism and harmony of your universe rise to consciousness as well? Why, might not all the stars of the morning sing together when they heard all the sons of men shouting for joy?" I acknowledge that these are not arguments. They are simply statements in language, by two clear-headed men not apt to deceive themselves, in a matter where they would not argue. I quote them, because I think what is needed most is to rescue the language in which we speak of God, the Infinite Spirit, from the language in which children might speak, or savages, — the language of idol worshippers, or of those who imprison God in a visible form. Let me just say this, and it shall be all. There is to me something amazing in that presumption which I meet now and then in the reviews, which really supposes that the thousand million men, more or less, who live in visible bodies in this little world are the only conscious beings in the infinite universe. It was absurd enough, in the days of men's ignorance, to suppose that sun, moon, planets, and stars all circled around this little globe of ours; absurd enough to suppose that sun and moon were set only to give us light, and that stars were set in constellations, only that men might exult in their beauty. But this absurdity is nothing to the arrogant insolence of the presumption which tells me that while I am conscious of my existence here, and look back with interest on my past and with curiosity on my future, the Power which makes me and sustains me, orders the sun to paint the lily for me, and bids the lily grow to be painted, is not conscious of His past, is not conscious of His present work, and is not curious about His future. This arrogance reaches its climax when we are told, as we so often are, that we men, forsooth, who are the lords of creation, are indeed its only conscious inhabitants. So many Alexander Selkirks, indeed, stranded on the edge of a desert.

> "I am monarch of all I survey.
> My right there is none to dispute."

But I do not ask you to engage in this high argument, which is, as I suppose, beyond logical reasoning. I wanted to say enough this morning, shall I say to justify our instinctive passion for flowers, and gardening, and nature, and the woods? I want to do honor to that nerve of the eternal life which runs through it all and makes its joy part, indeed, and element of the joy of God. This is no poor bit of the pleasure of sense alone. The passion that takes you out of doors is not one of the vulgar, selfish, or personal passions which Puritans were right in holding under lock and key. Here is the child of God who wants to know what his Father is doing. His own life quickens and warms and grows young as days grow longer and the sun rides higher, and it is in his godly nature and by one of the divine laws that he delights to see how other creatures of God are breaking from their wintry prison. Life seeks life and loves life. In the opening of a catkin of a willow, in the flight of the butterfly, in the chirping of a tree-toad or the sweep of an eagle, my life loves to see how others live, exults in their joy, and so far is partner in their great concern.

And this is really what we mean when we say what I think people generally understand, that a man is apt to be nearer to God when he is out of doors than when he is in his home. Literally, this might not be true. But what we are after is the larger life. We do not want to be limited wholly by things of the flesh, what we shall eat, what we shall drink. After these things the Gentiles seek, the Philistines most of all. What we do need is more of God. It may be some sudden and new hint of Him, it may be the infinite and perpetual lesson of the ocean or of the stars. Always it is life. Life larger than a room. Life larger than a day. It was when he got outside a room that the first man in the cool of the day walked with God. And for us, in these later days, it is that we may walk with God, more and more often, that the Saviour bids us " consider the lilies."

SERMONS OF THE WINTER,

FROM OCTOBER, 1892, TO JUNE, 1893.

BY

REV. EDWARD EVERETT HALE, D.D.

These sermons will be sent, post-paid, to any given address on receipt of price, six cents. Bound volume, $1.50.

No. 1. THE CHURCH AND THE WORLD.
" 2. THE FIRST CHURCH OF CHRIST.
" 3. LIFE HID WITH GOD.
" 4. THE PERFECT SUNDAY-SCHOOL.
" 5. TO GLORIFY GOD.
" 6. WHITTIER, CURTIS, LONGFELLOW.
" 7. "'TIS FIFTY YEARS SINCE."
" 8. PERSONAL RELIGION.
" 9. MODERN IDOLATRY.
" 10. TO ENJOY HIM FOREVER.
" 11. TRUTH.
" 12. HOW TO USE THE BIBLE.
" 13. LIGHT OF THE WORLD.
" 14. PHILLIPS BROOKS.
" 15. CREEDS AND LIFE.
" 16. LAW OF LOVE.
" 17. CHRISTIAN MYSTICS.
" 18. FAILURE AND STRENGTH.
" 19. PALM SUNDAY AND EASTER.
" 20. MANHOOD.
" 21. THE WILL OF GOD.
" 22. SUMMER SERVICE.

Subscriptions may be sent to the publishers,

J. STILMAN SMITH & CO.,
3 Hamilton Place, Boston.

THE STORY

OF

CHRISTOPHER COLUMBUS,

AS TOLD BY HIMSELF.

TRANSLATED AND EDITED BY

EDWARD EVERETT HALE, D.D.,

WITH THE STORY OF HIS LIFE FROM OTHER SOURCES
WHERE WE HAVE NOT HIS NARRATIVE.

For Sale by Booksellers.

Sent, post-paid, by the publishers on receipt of $1.25.

J. STILMAN SMITH & CO.,
3 Hamilton Place,
BOSTON.

www.ingramcontent.com/pod-product-compliance
Lightning Source LLC
Chambersburg PA
CBHW032047230426
43672CB00009B/1502